Writing Essentials

SECOND EDITION

A NORTON POCKET GUIDE

Dawn Rodrigues

UNIVERSITY OF TEXAS AT BROWNSVILLE

Myron C. Tuman

UNIVERSITY OF ALABAMA

 W • W • NORTON & COMPANY

New York • London

Printed in the United States of America

The text of this book is composed in ITC Stone Serif and Helvetica with the display set in Rockwell.
Composition by UG.
Manufacturing by Courier Companies.

Editors: Carol M. Hollar-Zwick, Jennifer Bartlett
Developmental Editor: Carol Flechner
Associate Managing Editor: Marian Johnson
Production Manager: Diane O'Connor
Editorial Assistant: Katharine Ings
Text Design: Joan Greenfield
Cover Design: Debra Morton-Hoyt

Library of Congress Cataloging-in-Publication Data

Rodrigues, Dawn.
     Writing essentials / Dawn Rodrigues, Myron C. Tuman. — 2nd ed.
        p.   cm. — (A Norton pocket guide)
     Includes index.

     ISBN 0-393-97336-0 (pbk.)

     1. English language—Rhetoric—Data processing—Handbooks,
manuals, etc.   2. Report writing—Data processing—Handbooks,
manuals, etc.   I. Tuman, Myron C., 1946–   .   II. Title.   III. Series.
PE1408.R6386   1998
808'.042'0285—dc21   98-34152
                                                                                            CIP

W. W. Norton & Company, Inc., 500 Fifth Avenue, New York, NY 10110
http://www.wwnorton.com

W. W. Norton & Company Ltd., 10 Coptic Street, London WC1A 1PU

     5 6 7 8 9 0

CONTENTS

ACKNOWLEDGMENTS

The authors wish to thank the following teachers for their thoughtful reviews of the manuscript: Jeremy Brigstocke, Santa Monica College; William Condon, University of Michigan; Louise Dibble, Suffolk County Community College; Beth L. Hewett, The Catholic University of America; Van E. Hillard, Duke University; Stephen E. Hudson, Portland Community College; Chandice M. Johnson, Jr., North Dakota State University; Nancy Montgomerey, Sacred Heart University; Bob Murray, Virginia Military Institute; Laurence E. Musgrove, University of Southern Indiana; James Raymond, The University of Alabama; Geoffrey Schmidt, Illinois Valley Community College; Carol Teel, George Washington University; Alison Warriner, Sacred Heart University; Holly Zaitchik, Boston University.

The production of a handbook is a little like that picture of modern-day surgery now a commonplace on TV dramas: with lots of people (all specialists of one sort or another) crowded around and working their magic upon a bit of exposed flesh or, in our case, text. While standard practice requires that one or more be singled out as authors, the successful completion of the operation is truly a collaborative process—in this instance, one that has been initiated and carefully monitored from the start by its original editor, Carol Hollar-Zwick, and is now under the watchful care of Jennifer Bartlett. And a special thanks to Kathryn Tuman for timely and thorough editorial assistance during the stifling summer of '98.

Writing Essays Online

1 Thinking, Writing, and Computers

Behind all writing lies the writer's interest in altering, if only slightly, some preexisting understanding or condition of the world. (Indeed, some would argue that such an interest in change lies behind all thinking.) Even a simple letter you might write home emerges from such an interest—possibly the practical interest in asking for money or the less immediate interest in informing family members about your activities, thus reaffirming your sense of belonging to an ongoing community. Likewise, most college writing assignments need to be thought of as an opportunity for you to alter readers' understanding by having them consider your own formal written presentation and explanation of events in the world.

Ideally, there is a natural connection between your having an interest in a topic and then writing about it: in such a situation, your text develops directly from your concern or interest.

In the real world, however, you often write not necessarily to express an interest in a topic, but to meet the demands of other people. As students, for example, you are regularly given writing assignments. But even when your writing is not directed by someone else, you may have little interest in the writing itself (for instance, when you write home to ask for money), or your interest in a topic may be strong but unfocused (for example, when you are outraged by a rate increase proposed by the local cable television company).

1a Thinking and the Writing Process

As noted above, thinking and writing are often connected by interest: you are angered by a proposed hike in cable-TV rates and decide to write a letter of protest. Here both your angry thoughts and your angry words use a common vocabulary organized into grammatical units to express ideas. We all think with words and express our thoughts when we write. Nevertheless, there is a fundamental difference between the two. In thoughts, words and associations come and go quickly, without much order or opportunity for development; in writing, our goal is to get everything—words, thoughts, examples, and so forth—in some sort of order: first things first, with everything else in its place, one item after the other, until the end. In a nutshell, thinking often seems easy; writing often seems hard.

The writing process described below attempts to bridge the gap between thinking and composing by encouraging you to work through your topic in repeated cycles of prewriting and exploration, drafting and organizing, rereading and revising. The hallmark of process-based writing classes is students regularly bringing drafts of their assignments to class for feedback from their classmates or teacher and then revising the pieces again for the next class.

1b Computers and the Writing Process

Computers offer an exciting way to bridge this gap between thinking and writing. Words on a computer screen, while not as fluid as those in our minds, are not nearly as fixed as those on paper. When you write by hand or type, words are entered and stored on the paper at once. Thus, editing such a text in order to change anything you have already said requires considerable effort, usually including rewriting or retyping. With word processing, the three acts of entering (or editing), printing, and saving the text are separate. You still use the keyboard to enter what you want to say, but now text is recorded in the computer's memory and reflected on its monitor, allowing you to alter it at will and, later, to print and save it (technically, to issue commands that send the text—called a file—to a printer and to a disk for storage).

Do not make the mistake of thinking that entering your writing into a computer, neatly saving it to disk, or sending it to a costly, high-quality laser printer somehow gives it any special value. The computer is strictly a tool that allows you to interact with your writing more easily, especially when it comes to improving what you have written by engaging in the ongoing process of revision.

Computers allow you an easy means of editing or otherwise revising (generally by deleting words or moving them from one location to another). Therefore, when you write with a computer, you can take more chances with your ideas, trying out new ways of thinking and expressing yourself throughout the brainstorming and drafting process. Indeed, writing with a computer is so fluid, in some ways so much like thinking, that the old categories of prewriting, drafting, and revising are no longer clear and distinct. Unlike traditional work, where each step takes place in a separate document, with word processing you can do all the work on a topic in a single file, deleting rough notes and early thoughts as the process proceeds.

1c Computers, Writing, and Risk Taking

The writing process gives all writers the opportunity to go from an unformed feeling about a subject to its full expression in a text. The computer helps writers during this period of struggle and uncertainty by offering them considerable technical support. With just a couple of keystrokes, old work can be copied and safely stored, freeing you to revise your position or even to try a new approach to the same topic without fear of losing something. Likewise, there is less pressure to get everything lined up from the beginning. You can easily write the conclusion first or add something to the introduction at the end. Network-based writing software offers even more help by allowing you to share your work with others, to receive feedback on what you have written, and, just as important, to see how others have responded to the current task. Computers take some of the work and anxiety out of composition, enabling you to give your writing energy and spontaneity.

2 Prewriting

Methods for discovering and gathering ideas are often called prewriting strategies. Prewriting refers to all the thinking, information gathering, and topic exploration that you do before you plunge into the first draft.

2a Exploring the Assignment

The best time to develop a risk-taking attitude is while thinking through the assignment. Most college writing will begin with a teacher-generated task that either defines your topic for you or instructs you to find a topic on your own. In either case, the assignment may also specify conditions about your audience and about your purpose in relation to that audience. Rarely, however, will a teacher be able to specify what it is about the topic that you find personally engaging.

Begin your work, therefore, by defining the assignment—es-

Exploring the Assignment

THE TOPIC

- What does the assignment ask me to do? What is its purpose? Is it to argue a position, to try to solve a problem, or to entertain the reader? Does it ask me to analyze, argue, report, or describe something? Does it require that I draw from my reading or other experience, or that I conduct research?
- Why am I considering writing on this topic? What am I expected to accomplish by writing this? What do I want to accomplish by writing this? What should the finished product look like?
- Does the assignment call for a certain genre or format such as a standard essay or research paper, letter to the editor, or editorial, or is it discipline-specific, calling for a format such as a proposal, memo, or lab report? How long must it be?
- Do I know enough about my topic? What do I need to do to learn more? Where will I be able to gather information—books, magazines, online sources, talking to others?

AUDIENCE

- Does this assignment have a specific audience? If so, who is it? How familiar will these readers be with my topic? What are their probable opinions? How familiar will my fellow students be with my topic? What are their probable opinions? If the readers of this piece were not in my class (and most papers are written for interested readers who have not sat in on your class discussions or done your assigned readings), would they still understand all my references?

INTEREST

- What aspect of the topic most interests me? Why?
- What is there in my own life (past, present, or future) that relates to this topic or helps to explain my interest in this topic?
- Can I use this personal connection in the paper itself to introduce, to help develop, or to draw conclusions about this topic?

pecially in terms of topic or content, audience, and purpose—all the time seeking for ways to strengthen your interest in this topic.

2b Group Discussion

Probably the most valuable form of prewriting is the easiest one—talking with others. By telling someone about your topic or discussing topic ideas with others, you have a chance to think through what you want to say before you begin to write.

ONLINE TIP ▶ Exchange Ideas in an Online Group Discussion

Many students have access to networked computer facilities that allow electronic discussion among students and teachers.

The most common program for such a purpose is electronic mail (E-mail), software that allows you to write messages to one or more people you identify in the "To" field of your message or to one or more groups, organized as distribution lists and so called since they automatically send a copy to each person on the list of any message sent to the list itself. Your class, for example, might be set up as a distribution list. E-mail messages, once printed or exported to regular text files that can be read and edited with a word processor, can then provide you with starting points or relevant details once you begin to draft your paper.

Finally, if you are reviewing Web pages as suggested in the online tip below ("Review Web Pages on Your Topic"), you can share what you have found by E-mailing to classmates the Web addresses (URLs or Uniform Resource Locators) of interesting sites you have located.

The "Online Tip" above offers suggestions for discussing your ideas online.

2c Prewriting with Computers

This section describes a number of practical, well-tested classroom techniques—all involving computers—for transforming your initial interest in a topic into writing that is both controlled and forceful.

BRAINSTORMING Brainstorming, a problem-solving technique, involves the spontaneous generation of ideas about a subject. To brainstorm, create a list of everything that comes into your mind about your subject. Write it all down as quickly as you can in the order that you think of it. To push yourself, set a time limit for yourself, such as ten minutes, or a number of items, such as fifteen.

SUBJECT: CENSORSHIP ON THE INTERNET

Censorship in print
E-mail and other private messages on the Internet
Hate groups and other political extremists on the Web
Censorship in other media (films, video, and television)
Community standards and defining obscenity

Increasingly, computers have access to the World Wide Web. Most software programs that are used to access the Web—*browsers*—have a button to initiate a search by a keyword, or you can go to one of the most helpful sites on the Web, Yahoo!, by using the "open" button, typing in "yahoo," and from there entering your keyword.

The Web is popular, in large part, because of the ease with which one can find information (admittedly not always the best or most accurate) and then move from site to site via hypertext linking—clicking on highlighted text to jump to another, related location.

Many Web pages also allow you to send E-mail messages for more information from the person or persons responsible for that page.

E-mail discussions and special-interest groups
Supreme Court ruling on Communications Decency Act
Responsibility of Internet service providers and other Internet-
    based companies
Internet-based research on sexuality
Chat groups and live interaction
Pornography on the Web

CLUSTERING Brainstorming is just a start. After you have finished brainstorming, consider using another prewriting strategy, clustering, to organize your ideas. **Clustering**, a technique for grouping similar items together, helps you collect your ideas and focus your thinking.

Read over your brainstorming list, and consider how related items could be grouped together—that is, clustered. Begin by putting a "1" next to the first item on the list. Then look for items similar to the first one, and put a "1" beside those items that match this item. Go to the next item on your list that does not have "1" beside it, and put a "2" next to it. Now proceed through your list, putting a "2" beside each similar item. Keep running down your list, using new numbers for items that do not fit into any existing clusters.

SUBJECT: CENSORSHIP ON THE INTERNET

1 Censorship in print
2 E-mail and other private messages on the Internet
3 Hate groups and other political extremists on the Web
1 Censorship in other media (films, video, and television)
1 Community standards and defining obscenity
2 E-mail discussions and special-interest groups

1 Supreme Court ruling on Communications Decency Act
2 Responsibility of Internet service providers and other
   Internet-based companies
3 Internet-based research on sexuality
2 Chat groups and live interaction
3 Pornography on the Web

So that you can see the results of your clustering, use the CUT and PASTE commands on your word processor to move the items into common groupings. Give each cluster grouping a name, compare the groups, consolidate similar items, add new items as they occur to you, and delete items that are no longer relevant. Clustering is a powerful tool for organizing your thoughts and for generating new ones. (You don't have to use all the items that appear on your brainstorming list. It is unlikely that all of your first ideas will fit into your paper.)

CLUSTER #1: CENSORSHIP ISSUES

- Censorship in print
- Censorship in other media (films, video, and television)
- Community standards and defining obscenity
- Supreme Court ruling on Communications Decency Act

CLUSTER #2: PERSON-TO-PERSON COMMUNICATION

- E-mail and other private messages on the Internet
- E-mail discussions and special-interest groups
- Responsibility of Internet service providers and other Internet-based companies
- Chat groups and live interaction

CLUSTER #3: OTHER INFORMATION

- Hate groups and other political extremists on the Web
- Internet-based research on sexuality
- Pornography on the Web

ONLINE TIP   Use Brainstorming and Clustering
to Generate and Organize Ideas

Use the Cut and Paste function of your word processor to group similar items from your brainstorming list into clusters. With the CAPS LOCK key depressed, type a heading or title for each cluster, and then use the Cut and Paste function again to rearrange entire clusters in logical order—for example, from most to least important or from most to least obvious.

FREEWRITING AND NUTSHELLING Freewriting means what the name implies: totally free writing, done without worrying about grammar, typing and spelling errors, paragraphing, or coherence. Write about anything at all or, if you have a specific assignment, about anything related to that assignment. Write for a specified time period, such as fifteen minutes, or until you have written a page or more.

After you have finished freewriting, read over what you have written, and summarize your ideas in a nutshell sentence, one that captures the gist of what you were trying to say in your freewriting.

Here is a sample of some freewriting done on the subject "Censorship on the Information Superhighway":

I wonder if pornography is as big a deal on the Web as people say. Are there really sexual predators lurking all around, trying to lure small children and others into danger? Are pornographic images all that easy to find, more so than on television or at the magazine racks in drug stores today? In some stores, adult magazines are stored behind the counter to keep them away from children. What is the high-tech equivalent of such an arrangement? Will adults be able to get to such materials on the Internet or will the whole thing be brought down to the level of broadcast television? And what about private discussions between adults—will this be protected on the Internet so that people are free to say what they want without fear of having their conversation made public?

After each freewriting session, read over what you have written, and write a summary or nutshell sentence. For example:

The new electronic forms of communication are raising many difficult questions about censorship and privacy.

Freewrite While You Draft to Generate New Ideas **ONLINE TIP**

Freewriting is especially productive with a computer because it is so easy to freewrite at any time during the writing process. If you are in the middle of a draft, trying to work out a particularly troublesome paragraph, just press ENTER a few times and begin freewriting right there—in the middle of your draft. If you come up with usable sentences, you can incorporate them into your draft by cutting and pasting the text.

> **ONLINE TIP**   Invisible Writing
>
> Invisible writing at the computer is freewriting with your monitor
> contrast turned down. To try invisible writing, turn down the
> brightness control so that the screen is completely dark. Type for
> fifteen minutes or so without stopping. Then read over what you have
> written to see if there is an idea, a phrase, or a particularly good
> sentence that you can use in your draft or develop further using one
> of the other prewriting strategies.

INVISIBLE WRITING   The point of invisible writing, or "writing blind," is to free writers from the urge to evaluate and revise their writing as they draft and to encourage them to let their ideas flow. You can try invisible writing at the computer by turning down your monitor contrast (see above), or you can try it with pencil and paper. To work with paper, you will need two sheets of notebook paper, one sheet of carbon paper, and a used-up ballpoint pen. Place the carbon paper between your two notebook pages. Use the empty ballpoint pen to do your writing. Although you cannot see what you are writing as you write, when you look at the second notebook sheet—the one beneath the carbon paper—you will see the results.

PAIRING OPPOSITES   Pairing opposites, especially what is commonly known about a subject and what is uncommon, is a prewriting strategy that can help you formulate an introduction as well as the main body to your paper. (See "Contrasting Attitudes," page 16.)

First, list what is commonly known about your subject—typical opinions and well-known or obvious information, including what less-informed students are likely to think about this topic. Then, list what is *not* commonly known about your topic—information that your readers are not likely to know or understand. In addition to settling on a topic for your essay, you may be able to use your list in your introduction, conclusion, or body paragraphs.

COMMON KNOWLEDGE ABOUT CENSORSHIP
ON THE INTERNET

There is talk in the media about protecting children who use
    computers.
Parents and schools are buying computers for children at record
    numbers.

There is already a wide variety of adult-oriented materials
available in print, television, video, and movies.

UNCOMMON KNOWLEDGE ABOUT CENSORSHIP
ON THE INTERNET

People may not know just what rights and limits they now have
regarding censored materials in print, television, video, or
movies.

People may not know just what steps governments and the
computer industry itself have already taken to protect children
using the Internet.

Taking the time to list the common and uncommon aspects
of your topic helps in another way: by listing what you imagine
your readers think about your topic, you are developing a
heightened sense of your audience.

Pairing Opposite Views **ONLINE TIP**

Any word processor will allow you to work with at least two columns
of running text on your screen. In the first column, you can develop
any one side of an argument—for example, arguments in favor of
a position or what most people think about this topic or what is
common knowledge about it. In the second column, you can consider
the other side: arguments against this position or what is unknown
about this topic.

When you are finished, read through your lists, and see if they
provide you with any insights into how you might develop your topic.

ANSWERING QUESTIONS Answering questions is a prewriting
technique that can be adapted to any topic. In the following
list of questions, just substitute your topic for the bracketed
areas—[ ].

1. How is [ ] commonly defined? Do my sources define [ ]
   differently? How am I defining [ ]? What are the major
   parts of [ ]?
2. What things appear similar to [ ], and how are they different from [ ]? What things that appear different from
   [ ] are nevertheless similar to it?
3. How does [ ] develop? What are the origins of [ ]? What
   conditions affect the growth of [ ]? What is the purpose
   of [ ]?
4. What do people in general have to say about [ ]? What

ONLINE TIP Use a Template File of Questions

A list of questions that you can answer as part of your prewriting can be stored either as a word processing file on a disk or as a Web page that you would open with a browser and then Copy and Paste back to your word processing document. If you have access to the Web, you can use the template questions on the *Writing Essentials* home page (www.wwnorton.com/WE), or you can create your own template file of questions by saving a set of prewriting questions as a word processing separate file. Each time you retrieve this file to begin generating ideas for a draft, *immediately save it as a new file.* Such a prewriting file for dialogical exploration might have separate paragraphs on the following topics: "Common Views of My Topic"/ "Uncommon Views of My Topic," or "Arguments in Favor of X"/ "Arguments Against X."

do experts have to say about [ ]? What is my personal experience with [ ]?

5. What are the conditions that make [ ] possible? How might those conditions be changed?

6. What do my readers know about [ ]? To what extent do I have to explain [ ] to them? How does their knowledge of [ ] affect the organization, style, and tone of my paper?

CHECKLIST 2 Prewriting Online

ON YOUR OWN
- Brainstorm ideas, or freewrite anywhere in your file.
- Select a prewriting assignment file that your teacher has made available.
- Create reusable prewriting files with your favorite prewriting questions.

WITH ACCESS TO E-MAIL OR COLLABORATIVE SOFTWARE
- Share any brainstorming or other lists you have generated with classmates by posting that work to the network.
- Read what classmates have suggested in their prewriting exercises, responding to their work through additional messages to individuals or to the group.
- Revise your original prewriting effort, and repost it to classmates.
- Copy helpful comments from classmates into your word processing file using the Block/Cut/Paste or Import features.

2d An Exploratory Draft

An **exploratory draft** is another means of discovering ideas. This draft, usually written before you have ample notes or a working outline, may be no more than a reflection of your random thoughts. Focus on putting your ideas into words, not on figuring out exactly what you want to say or where you want the paper to go. You can work on these and other organizational matters after you finish your exploration.

3 Organizing the Main Ideas

How do you move from prewriting to drafting? Much depends on your writing habits and preferences. Many writers see the writing process as an opportunity to think through the writing task in order to arrive at a full and often complex statement of their ideas and their opinions. Some writers prefer to plunge in with an exploratory, or discovery, draft—an extended, focused freewriting session that will need extensive reworking. Other writers prefer to write a carefully structured rough draft, using an outline to guide them as they write. Before you begin your structured draft, however, you should settle on a working thesis statement and do some preliminary planning.

If you have written one or more exploratory drafts or if you already have a clear sense of purpose and organization, you may be ready to produce a **rough draft**—a draft in which you lay out your ideas in a unified, well-developed, coherent essay. You can revise as you write, but when you have finished your "rough draft," it should be clear to a reader that you have taken time to work through your ideas. Thus, your rough draft should develop a clearly defined thesis statement in an orderly way with supporting paragraphs.

3a Formulating a Thesis Statement

A **thesis statement** is a sentence or group of sentences that presents the main idea, or the focus, of an essay. It is an assertion or opinion in need of explanation, support, or development—a position about the world that readers are unlikely to accept without elaboration or proof. View your thesis statement as a promise to your reader that your essay will develop the topic in the way that your thesis statement implies.

The thesis statement in college essays is often the last sentence of the introductory paragraph. To formulate a thesis statement, examine your prewriting for ideas that might grow into a focusing statement—if your word processing program allows it, possibly with the prewriting in one window and a draft of your paper in another. Aim to establish a working thesis statement that will help to channel your thinking before you begin drafting, but also recognize that many advanced writers have trouble identifying their true feelings about a subject until after they have done a considerable amount of thinking and even writing about that subject. Formulate a thesis to help you write a draft, but never feel obligated to use that thesis in your final draft. Indeed, a good place to look when you revise your thesis is at the conclusion or last paragraphs of your most recent draft. Writing really does help sharpen our thinking about a subject.

Sample Working Thesis Statements

FIRST TRY   Before the Internet, there were lots of different ways that the government shielded children from pornography while protecting the free-speech rights of adults. The rise of the Internet is calling many of these laws and practices into question.

SECOND TRY   The rise of the Internet is calling into question laws and traditions that for years have protected the free speech of adults while shielding children from pornography.

When should you write your thesis sentence? Some teachers recommend that students identify their thesis early in their writing processes. However, just because you have written a clear thesis statement does not mean that this is the topic in which you are genuinely interested. The best advice is to formulate a thesis early in your writing process but revise it regularly as your essay takes shape.

3b An Organizing Plan

Ideally, the organization of an essay should grow out of your thesis, the individual parts of your essay each representing a sensible means of developing the principal point you are making. If your organization does not follow your thesis, you have the option of reorganizing your major sections or reformulating your thesis.

With regard to organizing essays, it is important to realize that highly original, sophisticated essays can be based on simple, straightforward organizational plans in much the same way that dazzling houses can have simple floor plans. Indeed, one way to build something noteworthy is to start with a sound, uncomplicated plan. The two straightforward organizational methods described below can be varied and combined to form the structure for an almost unlimited number of essays.

CATEGORIES A categorical organizational plan entails dividing your main idea into smaller units that are both distinct and parallel—that is, where each subgroup or category presents a different point you are making yet one that is roughly equal to and about the same in importance as the other points you are making. An essay that is organized this way develops its central idea through a series of sections, each section supporting a point or subpoint of the thesis statement. Categorical development then can also work as a means of development within individual sections of a larger essay.

At various times, a short essay in this form, with three main subgroups or categories, each reduced to a single paragraph, along with an introductory and a concluding paragraph, has been labeled the **five-paragraph essay**. While there is clearly a danger in trying to divide or even reduce any topic into only three categories, especially when the categories overlap, categorical thinking remains an invaluable means (some would argue a necessary means) of thinking through complex subjects.

To use categorical organization effectively, you need to ask yourself the following questions; if you cannot answer "yes" to each of them, you may need to change the structure of your essay by reformulating your thesis or, more likely, reworking the steps you will be covering:

1. Is each of your points distinct, or are some merely restatements of others? A section on the right to free speech, for instance, is likely to overlap with separate sections on hate groups and political extremists on the Web.
2. Are your points roughly parallel, each point covering a comparable amount of material? If it turns out that you are much more interested in one point than in others, try working that point into your thesis and seeing if you can divide it into a series of new points.

3. Are the points presented in a sensible order—from first to last, least to most important, or, like a relay team, with the weakest link in the middle?
4. Do all points, taken together, accurately represent your overall position on your topic? If not, then ask yourself what your points taken together do represent, and reword your thesis accordingly.

CONTRASTING ATTITUDES   An essay developed by using contrasting attitudes supports its thesis by playing the common against the uncommon in the introduction. If, for example, you want to argue that censorship on the Internet is not really a new problem, then you could begin by noting what you assert to be the common view—that many people think that the Internet calls for new ways of dealing with objectionable material—and then continue, in your thesis statement and in the development of your essay, by noting the uncommon attitude—that the problems posed by the Internet and censorship are the same ones that societies have dealt with for hundreds of years: protecting children while granting more freedom to adults. You could also use the common/uncommon structuring principle to present the opposite view—first noting in the introduction that for years people have managed to achieve a balance between giving freedom to adults while protecting children but that now, with the rapid, largely unregulated growth of the Internet, this process of control and restraint seems to be breaking down. Similarly, by starting with a portrayal of all the current forms of censorship, you could argue that the Internet offers us liberation from all censorship.

The overall structure of an essay based on the contrasting-attitudes method of organization will vary, depending on whether you want to focus exclusively on either the common or the uncommon view of your topic or whether you want to devote the first few paragraphs of your essay to the opposing viewpoint before turning to your side of the issue. Again, your position may be the common one or the uncommon one. In the first few paragraphs of your essay, however, you may want to explain that you understand why some people hold a different view.

COMBINING CATEGORIES AND CONTRASTING ATTITUDES The techniques of categorical organization and contrasting attitudes can be combined in most essays. The thesis that censorship on the Web reflects society's interest in protecting children might be developed by listing several reasons for your belief, each of which might be developed further by discussing some variation of contrasting attitudes. For example, at one point in your larger argument about the dangers of the Internet, you could include several paragraphs that present the opposing argument—that here, finally, is a communications medium that will or should allow people to interact without any interference from third parties. Then you could move back to your main argument, perhaps to a paragraph that discusses how a properly regulated Internet will create a truly safe environment for children to explore the world. Even this strategy could be expanded by listing the ways in which regulations could protect even the rights of children to some degree of privacy.

3c A Working Outline as a Drafting Aid

To provide some structure during your drafting sessions, consider creating a minimal, flexible outline with your word processor. Instead of using fixed, numbered headings and subheadings, type an informal list, and rearrange the items as your draft develops. Indent to add subheadings and details. As you write, you can freely add, delete, review, or move entire outline sections.

Use an Outline Template to Help Generate a Draft ◀ ONLINE TIP

Create an idea-generating outline template such as the one below. When you draft your essay, open a second document with a copy of the outline template in it and with a draft of your document in the first window. Use your informal outline to get started, but allow yourself the freedom to alter your ideas as you write. After a few hours of drafting, revise your outline to match the current shape of your essay.

SAMPLE OUTLINE TEMPLATE
Introduction and Thesis:
  Key Idea:
    Supporting Points: (*examples to come*)
  Key Idea:
    Supporting Points:
  Key Idea:
    Supporting Points:

3d Paragraph Structure

The flexible combination of categories and contrasting attitudes, discussed above, also provides the basis for effective individual paragraphs. Like essays, most paragraphs should have a topic (called a topic sentence) and supporting information arranged in a logical way. A topic sentence (not always the first sentence) gives the reader some indication of what the rest of the paragraph will cover and may also provide the reader with a clue as to how the material will be developed. In this paragraph, for instance, the second sentence gives you an indication of the paragraph's topic.

Try to develop paragraphs that coincide with the purpose of your essay. For example, an essay explaining the importance of selecting the right college might include different kinds of paragraph patterns. One topic sentence might state that public universities and private colleges provide students with vastly different experiences; this paragraph would be developed best by using a contrasting-attitudes pattern. If, later in the same essay, you want to isolate some key differences between these types of school, you could list these differences in a separate paragraph.

Paragraphs can also be used as transitional devices, to guide readers from one line of thought to another. Such a paragraph might briefly summarize what has gone before (in this case, that paragraphs themselves are key organizational units in developing an essay) while pointing forward to the next topic.

4 Framing the Main Ideas

Three key parts of an essay—the title, introduction, and conclusion—should work together to frame or support the organizing structure discussed in section 3. The introduction prepares readers for the thesis, the conclusion announces the end of the essay's development, and the title gives readers a handle to the whole thing.

4a The Introduction

The introduction is your opportunity to capture your readers' attention and interest them in what you have to say. An effective way of introducing a piece of writing is by establishing some common ground between you and your readers, leading

Drafting Strategies

- Develop a working outline from the ideas you have generated in early freewriting or prewriting activities. Use your outline to guide you as you make your draft, but remain open to fresh insights and ideas that occur to you as you work. If your outline is on computer, you can easily revise it to conform with any new direction your writing is taking.
- Read over your emerging draft regularly, especially when you start a new drafting session. Rereading both refreshes your memory about the content of your text and gives you a sense of how you need to adjust the evolving structure.
- Begin anywhere to get started—the end, the middle, wherever you want. Don't feel that you have to draft your essay in the same order that readers will read it.
- Try using the categories and contrasting-attitudes strategies to help you get unstuck. Ask yourself, "Can I add a parallel example or illustration in the next paragraph?" Or "Do I want to introduce a contrast to what I have just written?"

up to your singling out one aspect of this common ground that needs closer study or reconsideration—the thesis statement. Some writers like to wait until after they have finished a draft before writing an introduction; other writers find that, having written the introduction, they have established sufficient momentum to write the rest of the essay. Although you will want to create an introduction that fits your topic, at times you may find it difficult to get started. If you get stuck, try the prewriting strategy that asks you to pair common and uncommon attitudes about your topic, or see the sample introductions, below.

Sample Introductions

CURRENT ATTITUDES   State what many people think, followed by the thesis statement.

> ▶ Many people think of computing as a wholesome activity for their children. They purchase an expensive computer system at Christmas and are happy when eight-year-old Johnny spends hour after hour at the screen. [*Thesis*] Little do they realize just how much unregulated adult content is currently available to children on the Internet.

POSSIBLE SOLUTIONS   State alternatives; then suggest one solution as the thesis statement.

> ▶ The free expression of ideas has long been a goal of American life. Some people point to the New England town meeting as the model of such openness. Others point to a free, independent press. Still others point to the library system or to the widespread access to television. [*Thesis*] Today, many people are starting to realize that it is the personal computer that finally offers the greatest hope for democracy.

DIRECT ANNOUNCEMENT   Begin immediately with the thesis statement.

> ▶ [*Thesis*] The personal computer hooked to the Internet finally offers the possibility of expression of ideas free of government interference. *Or* [*Thesis*] The personal computer hooked to the Internet has become a chief threat to traditional family life.

QUESTIONS   Start with a question or a series of questions, followed by the thesis statement.

> ▶ Where do you want to go today? a Microsoft commercial asks. Is it to engage in a serious discussion about human sexuality? Do you wish to find some crucial information about AIDS prevention or possibly to view classic works of art portraying nude men and women? [*Thesis*] If so, the U.S. Congress, through the Communications Decency Act, might be interested in curtailing your activities.

ANECDOTE   Start with a brief anecdote, followed by the thesis statement.

> ▶ It is 3:30 in the afternoon, and twelve-year-old Jan is home alone after school, working on her computer. Only she is not doing her homework or even playing a video game. She is instead chatting and occasionally flirting with a virtual room full of strangers. [*Thesis*] The computer revolution enables an unprecedented level of private and explicit conversation between children and adults.

ALLUSION   Start with a reference to another work, followed by the thesis statement.

> ▶ In Orwell's *1984*, there are television screens and television cameras everywhere. Regardless of where Winston Smith

goes, ... [*Thesis*] Today's government seems just as intent on monitoring our private, computer-based communications.

DEFINITION   Start with a definition, and follow it with the thesis statement.

► Censorship refers to the monitoring of personal activities by the state or some comparable institution of social control. In recent years, the state exercised this control mainly over what was broadcast into the home via television. . . . [*Thesis*] The Internet is now raising a host of new issues related to state censorship of information available in the home.

UNRELATED FACTS   Start with a series of facts, followed by the thesis statement, which promises to pull those facts together.

► The local malls are nearly deserted. Happy hour at the town's favorite watering hole is no longer drawing a crowd. There are no lines at the movie theater. [*Thesis*] Everyone, it seems, is at home, trying to find his or her heart's desire on the Internet.

QUOTATION   Start with a brief quotation, followed by an explanation of the quotation and a link to the thesis statement.

► Recent government actions to curtail free speech on the Internet has reminded many people of the saying "Eternal vigilance is the price of liberty." The Internet offers Americans the opportunity to discuss issues freely and without government interference, yet [*thesis*] it is unlikely that we will be able to maintain this freedom without a great deal of effort.

4b The Conclusion

A strong conclusion commonly restates your thesis in different language or from a fresh viewpoint and then widens the implications and scope of the thesis. An effective conclusion will often echo the introduction. One advantage of having a distinctive introduction—for example, beginning with the image of governments of the past trying to censor information as in banning or even burning books, or of television cameras following Orwell's Winston Smith—is that you have something strong and colorful to return to at the end of your paper—an image of government censors rounding up and dumping home computers, or of a contemporary, less gloomy Winston Smith zapping Big Brother with the remote control while surfing the

Web. Thus, such references to the opening give readers a sense
of completion.

What you should not do in the conclusion, however, is introduce new topics.

4c The Title

While some writers like to come up with a title before they write
their essay, it may be more helpful to wait until you have finished a draft and have an effective opening. The best places to
look for a title are in the opening and concluding sentences of
your essay. Ideally, the title, the introduction, and the conclusion should all work together, and when you come up with a
good idea for one, you can often extend this idea to include the
other two. A paper on censorship on the Internet that begins
with a reference to book burning, for example, could play with
this image—"Electronic Book Burning," if you are opposed to
recent government attempts at censorship.

Good titles should be brief, informative, and engaging. An
acceptable title for a paper on the problems of regulating adult
content on the Internet might hint at both positive and negative features: "Making the Internet Family-Friendly." The title
becomes more engaging with a colorful allusion, "For Adults
Only: Making the Internet Family-Friendly," and perhaps more
effective still when shortened to "The Internet: For Adults
Only?" with the question mark indicating the open-ended
nature of the debate. Either title with a reference to the half-hidden "adult only" world could then provide material for
both your introduction and conclusion.

If you get writer's block whenever you try to think of titles,
consider starting a "Title" file, in which you jot down title ideas
that occur to you at any point during your writing course.

5 Revising

Revising is an important part of the writing process and is ideally suited for word processing; you can easily alter your text
and move it from one place to another. Even though you may
do a lot of revising while you draft with a word processor, your
initial goal should be to generate a draft. When you have decided that your draft covers what you want to say, then you

Building Files for Future Reference ❮ ONLINE TIP

Setting aside special files can help you organize and keep track of information you consult frequently as you write. Create the files below, or come up with variations of these to suit your purposes.

"GREAT IDEAS" FILE
Use this file to tuck away ideas that might be useful in the essay you are currently working on or that might fit into another essay.

"TITLES" FILE
Use this file to collect titles that fascinate you. Include good titles written by others as well as those you dream up yourself.

"ERRORS" FILES
Each time you have a paper returned to you with errors indicated, put the errors into this file for future reference. And remember to correct the errors in the file, too. Look at the file when you revise your paper to avoid making the mistake again. For more ideas on tracking errors, see the Online Tip on page 181.

"INTRODUCTIONS" AND "CONCLUSIONS" FILES
Collect interesting introductions and conclusions that you might use as models for your own work, or save introductions and conclusions you have written that you especially like.

may focus on revision. Be sure to allow some time between completing the first draft and revising it; if you begin revising too soon, you may be too close to your material to be able to look at it critically.

5a Revising on Your Own

It is important to keep your readers in mind throughout the revising process. Read your paper thoughtfully, imagining that you are a naive but interested reader, one who has no specialized knowledge about your topic but who is eager to learn.

This is a good time to print your draft, drawing lines through sentences that need to be deleted and inserting new sentences to make your ideas flow smoothly, while indicating where you want to move paragraphs so that they are at their most effective locations. If you are revising directly at the computer, be sure to save your file with a new name before you begin to make changes. Instead of drawing arrows and marking sections for later revision, use the Cut and Paste function to experiment with rearranging paragraphs, sentences, and words.

Even if you do most of your revision at the computer, you will want to print out and revise a version on paper as well. Reading the same text in a different medium can help distance you from your ideas so that you may see your work more objectively and revise more effectively. Accordingly, you may want to read your paper aloud.

CHECKLIST 4   **On-Your-Own Revision Questions**

- Where would a reader get lost?
- What do I need to change to make my ideas clearer for a reader?
- Where do I need to create new paragraphs? If I create new paragraphs, do I need to make changes to the newly created paragraphs?
- Can my reader follow the movement of paragraphs? (*Note:* If not, try adding transitional sentences or phrases to guide the reader.)
- Do my paragraphs connect directly with my thesis statement?
- Do the sentences in each paragraph flow smoothly from one sentence to the next? If not, I will need to do some revising. (*Note:* Sometimes you can make sentence-by-sentence changes; other times you may need to recast an entire section. You can press ENTER a few times and do some trial revising in your document.)
- Is each paragraph adequately developed? If not, I may need to do more research to gather sufficient information. (*Note:* When you do have the information, move your cursor to wherever you need to add that information, and start typing.)
- Would a different introduction or conclusion strengthen my paper?

5b Group Workshopping

At some point in the writing process, all writers benefit by being able to share their work with others and, if possible, to read what others have written on the same or a comparable topic. While students can share their work informally outside the class, many teachers hold revision workshops in their classes. The most important aspect of such group workshops is the opportunity they offer you to read your classmates' work and, thus, to get a better sense of what goes into writing an effective paper.

CHECKLIST
5

Group-Workshop Revision Questions

OVERALL
- Which paper(s) do you like best? Why?
- Which has the most effective introduction? The strongest conclusion? Why?
- Which has the most compelling main point? Can you state this point in one sentence?
- How does your sentence match the thesis sentence in this paper?

COHERENCE AND ORGANIZATION
- Which paper makes it easy for you to follow the main ideas?
- Can you identify the parts of the paper and some of the transitions the writer uses to move smoothly from one section to another?
- Are key terms defined?

AUDIENCE
- Is the paper intended for a specialized or a general audience?
- Does it contain references to people, works, and ideas that would be unclear to its intended audience?

STYLE AND SENTENCE STRUCTURE
- Are most of the sentences straightforward, with concrete subjects followed by action verbs?
- Can you identify any particularly effective sentences?
- Are there other noteworthy aspects of any of the other papers that should be mentioned?

All papers have strengths and weaknesses, yours included. But in any group of papers, one or more will stand out as being more effective than the others. Always try to read at least three of your classmates' papers, and then ask yourself which ones work best and why? What, if anything, do these papers accomplish that could help you in revising your own paper? Which ones have a clear thesis and sense of development? Lots of compelling details? Good transitions? The most interesting title and introduction? The best conclusion? Use the questions in Checklist 5 to guide you.

If you have the opportunity, share your thoughts with your group, constantly seeing if you can detect reasons for the amount of agreement or disagreement within the group. If you do not have this opportunity, use what you like best in your classmates' work as a basis for revising your own work. Modeling your work on someone else's, trying to express your

ONLINE TIP ▶ Group Workshopping

If the software on your school's network allows you to share files, you can take part in group-workshop or peer-review sessions at different times of the day or week.

1. Save your work to the network so that it is available to your classmates.
2. Bring up each of your classmates' papers on your screen. If you are working in a group, read all of the papers on which you are supposed to comment.
3. Split the screen, and open a new window in which you can write. Using the revision questions in Checklist 5, comment on the papers as a group, being critical but kind and helpful. When you are finished, either print out your comments and share them with the group, or, if possible, post your comments to the network so that others can view and respond to them.

thoughts in the same clear fashion that a classmate does, is a basic component of learning and not at all the same as using someone else's ideas (see " Avoiding Plagiarism," section 9e).

5c Peer Editing

In peer editing, you closely read another student's paper. As with group workshopping, it is always helpful to focus on what your partner needs to do to improve his or her paper. As a peer reader, phrase criticism carefully, remembering to be constructive. Begin your comments with a positive statement to the student whose paper you have read. Focus on questions of content and organization, saving minor points, such as grammatical errors, for last. (Better yet, postpone talking about grammatical and typographical errors until a later session.) Use questions such as those in Checklist 6 to guide you.

5d Proofreading

When you have revised your paper to your satisfaction, you need to take time for final proofreading, locating and correcting mechanical and typographical errors. Make sure you go

Peer-Editing Revision Questions

OVERALL
● What do you like best about the essay?

INTRODUCTION
● Do the opening lines of your partner's essay engage you? Why or why not?

THE MAIN IDEA
● What is the point of the essay?

COHERENCE
● Are there any places where you get lost?
● Can you suggest a revision?

ORGANIZATION
● Are the paragraphs well developed?
● What would you like to see expanded in the essay?

CONCLUSION
● Does the conclusion summarize or point forward?
● Can you suggest improvements?

OTHER CONCERNS (AUDIENCE, SENTENCE STRUCTURE, EMPHASIS, ETC.)
● Are there any other aspects of this paper that work well?

through your paper several times, each time reading for one of the following purposes:

● To check paragraph structure
● To check sentence structure and sentence errors
● To run a spell check and to read to check spelling
● To check typographical errors
● To check word choice and usage

A word of caution: Do not substitute the use of a spell checker for a thorough proofreading. Spell checkers will not pick up usage problems or words that are mistyped but are still words (such as *he* for *the*). Also, read your paper in different media—several times on-screen and several times on paper. Errors that go undetected in one medium are often easy to spot in another.

- Use computer error-checking tools cautiously. Many word processing programs have grammar and style checkers built in to help you as you revise. They are less reliable than spell checkers, flagging items that may be correct while missing other problems.
- Check sentence and paragraph structure by moving the cursor through each paragraph one sentence at a time. Press ENTER if you find that you have shifted topics and may need a new paragraph. (You can return to this spot later and make a final decision.)
- Use your word processor's Search option to help you locate those places that you have marked on your printed draft and want to change on the screen.
- Use your word processor's Search function to locate instances of a particular kind of usage error, such as confusing *to*, *too*, and *two*, or *they're*, *their*, and *there*. Search for each word, and check to see if you have used it correctly. To correct an error, just type in the change.
- Run your paper through the spell checker, but remember that spell checkers do not catch all errors. Read your paper carefully before you turn it in.
- Proofread online by starting at the bottom of your file and reading backward, one sentence at a time, so that you do not get caught up in the flow of your ideas.
- Change the font of your paper on-screen or view it in a preview mode to make your paper look different and to help you spot errors.

Research

6 Search Strategies for Gathering Information

A research paper, like an essay, solves a problem or presents a point of view and, like an essay, needs to be planned, organized, and developed. Although some research papers require the same kind of idea-generating strategies that are used in essays, most research projects require you to develop strategies for gathering, evaluating, and interpreting information. A key difference between writing a research paper and writing a personal essay is that when you do research, your understanding of your topic will often undergo significant changes as you gather information and reflect on what you have written. As a result, you must test your thesis as your research progresses and revise when necessary.

In the electronic age, information gathering includes searching print sources as well as online sources and using computers to store and retrieve the results of a search. Although most libraries are gradually replacing printed indexes like the familiar *Readers' Guide to Periodical Literature* with online versions that can be searched more efficiently, you may need to continue using print indexes for many more years to search for older materials such as what film critics had to say about George Lucas's *Star Wars* when it was first released in 1977. When working with current or recent topics such as welfare reform or immigration policy, the available electronic tools streamline your information-gathering processes. Within minutes, you should be able to locate many current articles and Web sources on your topic, often in full-text form.

This chapter integrates traditional advice on research writing with advice for using appropriate technologies throughout the research process. Because of the changing nature of research, you need to take special care in organizing your research results using your computer so that you can take advantage of the flexibility that technology offers.

6a Research Questions and Key Words

Before you begin gathering information for a research paper, explore your topic by answering questions such as the following or those on pages 11–12:

- What aspects of the topic interest me?
- What do I already know about this topic?
- What would I like to find out?

After you do some background reading on your topic, ask yourself questions such as these:

- How does my new learning affect my original research question(s)?
- What do I need to learn?
- Where can I find this information?

Then formulate some early research questions based on your topic, such as the following, which were used by the author of the research paper on pages 51–54:

- Should certain areas of the Web be limited to adults?
- Is it technically feasible to block indecent sites from children?
- Is it possible to block offensive areas without limiting freedom of speech?
- What groups are in favor of limiting free speech on the Web?
- What are their reasons for their position?

As you answer your research questions, begin listing **key words**—terms that are related to your emerging topic. You will be able to use these key words when you search for information. In the paper examining censorship issues on the Web, a preliminary key-word list might include the following terms and synonyms:

TERM	SYNONYM OR ALTERNATE TERM
Web censorship	Internet censorship
Surf-patrol software	Cyber-patrol software
First amendment	Freedom of speech
Control of information	Censorship

6b The Online Catalog and Other Library Holdings

Most libraries have **online catalogs** in addition to or in place of traditional card catalogs. Unfortunately, most cataloging

software is unique to a particular library or to a regional or state
wide library system. As a result, when you search in the library
catalogs of different institutions, you will most likely learn the
mechanical process for searching each catalog.

Your institution may have a wide variety of online full-text
databases available to registered students. If so, you may be able
to locate useful resources related to your topic in online aca
demic journals or in national newspapers. But don't make the
mistake of limiting yourself to what you can access online. Use
all the resources at your disposal, including the books and ref
erence resources in your library as well as the books and journal
articles available to you from other libraries through interli
brary loan.

Your library's catalog may list both books and **serial hold
ings**. (The term *serial* refers to magazines, journals, newspapers
and other publications that are published at regular intervals.
If serials are not cross-referenced in the online catalog, you will
need to consult a **serials list**, a computer-generated list of the
periodicals and journals that your library subscribes to in print
format. Usually there are many copies of the serials list available
near the computers or computer terminals in your library. After
you determine whether your library has the serial you want
you need to locate it in the periodicals section of your library

SUBJECT VERSUS KEY-WORD SEARCHING   Electronic catalog
can be searched by author, title, subject, and—in many
cases—key word. The terms *subject* and *key word* refer to differ
ent things. If you search by subject in your library catalog, you
may need to use the correct Library of Congress subject heading
since **subject searching** retrieves those holdings that are clas
sified under specific headings. **Key-word searching** is more
comprehensive. If you search by key words, you locate all the
sources in your library that include the key words in the title
or in the abstract. For example, if you are searching for infor
mation on *censorship*, which is a valid Library of Congress sub
ject heading, you will get a list of holdings related to that term
But if you type in *information control*, you will not get any results
since *information control* is not a valid subject heading. *Note:* I
the default (built-in) setting in the library catalog you are using
is set to Subject search, you may need to click on Key Word to
change the setting.

Some periodical indexes and subscription databases develop
their own lists of subject headings: for example, Medline and

the Educational Resources Information Center (ERIC) both use subject headings that they have developed independent of the Library of Congress Information System.

USING THE LIBRARY OF CONGRESS SUBJECT HEADINGS

1. Look up a word or phrase related to your topic in the *Library of Congress Subject Headings (LCSH)*, a large book that is usually found at the reference desk in your library. If the word or phrase is printed in boldface type, you have a term that is a valid subject heading. (Alternately, go to the Library of Congress Web, and select LOCIS (Library of Congress Information System). Next select Subject Headings.
2. If the word or phrase appears in lightface type, look at the cross references that follow USE for valid *LCSH* subject headings.
3. Select from the cross references following USE a word or phrase that is closest to the particular subject about which you need information (for example, Censorship—USE book censorship, intellectual freedom, books—censorship).
4. You will notice BT (broader term), RT (related term), and NT (narrower term) before some of the words. These are cross references to related subject headings (for example, NT Book Burning; RT Challenged Books; BT Literature and Morals).

6c Standard References and Indexes

You can begin your search for background information with standard library references, bibliographies, or periodical indexes—either print or online (CD-ROM or subscription databases accessible through the Web). Depending on your topic, you can also begin your search with the Web-based versions of these standard resources.

STANDARD LIBRARY REFERENCES Whether you use your library or the Web, begin your research by consulting such print or electronic references as the *Oxford English Dictionary* or *Webster's Third New International Dictionary of the English Language* for definitions of any unfamiliar terms. You might also want to consult the *World Almanac and Book of Facts*, the *World Book Encyclopedia*, or *Grolier International Encyclopedia* for background information on your topic. These sources provide summaries of the general information that many educated readers may already possess and can be used to increase your own knowledge.

Note: These valuable references are normally not available on the Web unless your library has subscribed to them for registered students.

SPECIALIZED REFERENCES   As a rule, your status as an expert will be enhanced if, in your writing, you cite specialized sources rather than general ones. Your library may have many specialized references on specific topics, such as African American literature, mythology, birding, or medieval history. To search for a list of references on your topic, try typing [*your topic*] and *ref* in the Key Word field of your online catalog (for example, *birding ref*).

BIBLIOGRAPHIES   You may want to begin your reading by consulting one or more sources listed in an index such as the *Bibliographic Index*, which gives entire bibliographies on your topic. If you are searching the Web, search for [*your topic*] *bibliography*, and you may receive a list of items related to your topic (for instance, *African American bibliography*).

SPECIALIZED PERIODICAL INDEXES   Your library may have some indexes that provide you with listings of sources in periodicals focusing on your discipline. Ask a librarian to help you locate the databases available to your institution. The following indexes may be available in print, on CD-ROM, or on the Web (either free or by institutional subscription).

ABI/INFORM
Art Index
CARL UnCover (Colorado Alliance of Research Libraries)
Education Index
ERIC (Education Resources Information Center)
Humanities Index
Modern Language Association Index
Science Citation Index
Social Science Citation Index
Social Sciences Index

1. Learn how to search your own library's online catalog. Find out if you can search by key word as well as by subject, author, and title. Determine whether you have to change any settings to do a key-word search and whether you can do Boolean searching. (See page 38.)
2. Find out if you can access other library catalogs through your catalog. (If your library is part of a statewide system, its catalog may be linked to other libraries.) Find out if you have checkout privileges at any of these libraries.
3. Learn how to search for books in several other libraries. You can reach these libraries through the following gateways:

    Libraries: from Yahoo!
    ⟨http://www.yahoo.com/Reference/Libraries/⟩

    Library of Congress Home Page
    ⟨http://lcweb.loc.gov/⟩

4. If your library does not have a list of discipline-specific reference books, try searching for [*your topic*] *ref*, replacing *your topic* with a key word related to your research. For example, if you are looking for reference information on censorship, search for *censorship ref*. You should receive a list of reference works available in your library on censorship.

6d The World Wide Web

The World Wide Web is the latest and best-known advancement of an earlier global, interconnected network of computers called the Internet. Originally designed to enable defense researchers at different institutions to share data, in the form of the World Wide Web it has fast grown into a resource used for business, education, and entertainment. The Web includes collections of information assembled by faculty and students at different institutions, by government officials, by social-service agencies, and, increasingly, by specific businesses or industries.

The information assembled on the Web can be accessed through home pages—files that contain hypertext links (sometimes called hyperlinks) to text, images, sounds, or video. When you click on a link—usually a blue underlined word or phrase—the computer connects you to the page on which the information is stored. The links can lead to files on your local computer or to a specific home page (or even a section of a home page) on a computer located anywhere in the world. To access Web pages, you use a program called a browser. Netscape Navigator and Internet Explorer are the two most common browsers available.

Much information that is useful in your research will be found on home pages developed by various organizations and publishing groups: online journals, college classes, businesses government agencies, and nongovernment organizations (NGOs). The information at each site represents the views of the authors of that specific site. Each site will have a different bias; NGOs represent partisan viewpoints and should be used with care.

ADDITIONAL SOURCES OF INFORMATION   Other sources of information on the Web include the many mailing lists (Listserv or ListProc), forums, or newsgroups that have been formed on topics ranging from art and beekeeping to censorship issues to zoology. Recent submissions to these "living databases" can be searched using DejaNews, ⟨http://www.dejanews.com⟩, but unless the newsgroup or mailing list has developed archives to store older messages, your readers may not be able to retrieve your sources.

You can also use the Web for standard sources of information, including newspapers around the world, current newsmagazines and journals (often just sample stories—for back issues, you may need a subscription), government information, thesauruses, almanacs, encyclopedias (some require subscriptions—check to see if your school has bought one), refereed academic journals accessible with or without passwords, and online books.

If you are doing an online research project drawing on an online source, you can create a hyperlink to it for the convenience of readers who may not have access to the print publication. (You should realize, however, that given the restrictions in the copyright law, you may not be using the latest or best edition of a book that is available in print.)

Online collections are available at the following sites:

U of Virginia
Gutenberg collection
The Bartleby Collection

You can find some selections and occasionally whole chapters of current books at selected bookstores on the Web. These are designed to entice you so that you will purchase the books. *Note:* It is a violation of copyright law to print and share these chapters with others.

SEARCHING THE WEB Unlike libraries, which are organized according to the Library of Congress system of classification, the Web has not developed any standard for categorizing works. Contributors to the Web publish separate pages or sets of pages without providing a category to which these pages should be linked. As a result, finding information on the Web requires skill and patience.

Learn how to use several of the **search engines**, computer programs that look for sites to match the key words you type into a selection box. InfoSeek, Alta Vista, and Lycos are some of the most popular. Websites such as Yahoo! provide search capabilities, even though they are more appropriately considered **subject directories**, collections of topics that permit you to browse and review. Some search engines allow you to use **Boolean search operators**—*and*, *not*, and *or*—to broaden or narrow your search, thus making it more likely that you will be able to locate useful information.

If you develop a list of search terms and a list of synonyms or related terms, you can then explore different combinations of terms in an effort to find the best resources available. Let's say that your topic is "Web censorship." Although you search for books on censorship in your library catalog, you are not likely to find entire books on that topic. But in your effort to locate material on censorship, you might come across the book *Censorship and Intellectual Freedom*. As a result, you could add *intellectual freedom* to your list of search terms.

Using Search Engines **ONLINE TIP**

SEARCH ENGINES

WebCrawler   www.webcrawler.com
Flexible, powerful engine that gives summaries or simple lists.

Yahoo!   www.yahoo.com
Especially good for browsing. Customize your search results using ⟨www.edit.my.yahoo.com⟩.

HotBot   www.hotbot.com
Allows you to search specific domains, such as .edu, .com, or .org.

Infoseek   www.infoseek.com
One of the fastest search engines on the Web.

Alta Vista   www.altavista.digital.com
Offers the most extensive coverage of sites.

- Start with a broad topic. On the Web, you may discover excellent "pathfinder" (general) sites that other people have developed. In the library, a general search often results in books that provide excellent background information as well as suggestions for key words that you can use in subsequent searches.
- To find a topic or to narrow a broad topic, browse the Web using a search tool such as InfoSeek or a subject directory such as Yahoo!, which includes various subject categories that you can explore at your leisure. Note what words or terms are used to describe concepts or ideas about your topic.
- Examine one or two key books on your topic to determine further what words are used to describe concepts in this field of study.
- Develop a list of search terms that includes synonyms or related terms. If you are writing about illegal immigration, you might search for *border patrol agents* and *illegal immigration*. If your results yield discussions of fraud among border patrol agents, you can conduct a new search for *border patrol* and *fraud*.
- Search in various databases using the same terms as well as any new terms that seem relevant. Keep a list of key words and subject heading for future searches.
- Use Boolean operators (*and*, *or*, and *not*) to combine terms and control the nature of the items you retrieve.
  - Use *and* between words to limit your search to those holdings that include both (*Web and censorship*).
  - Use *or* between words to expand the results of your search. If similar terms are used to describe your topic, you might want to include a list of synonyms in your search request (*Mexican American or Chicano or Latino and literature*).
  - Use *not* to eliminate false "hits." For example, a search for help in writing college compositions could begin with *composition not music*.

6e Integrating Library and Web Searches

Adapt your search techniques to your specific needs. If your library's collection is accessible through a Web browser, you can move interchangeably between library searching and Web searching. If a preliminary search of the library catalog suggests that your topic is too current to be included in it, you may want to move temporarily to the Web before returning to library-catalog searching. However, keep in mind that if your assignment requires academic research in your subject area, then you probably need to start with traditional library sources and supplement them with carefully selected Web resources.

You may want to do some preliminary browsing in a library catalog, online periodical index, or the Web. A good place to browse in the library is in the stacks, near the Library of Congress number for your subject area. Take a few books off the shelf, and page through them to get a general sense of how writers treat this topic. On the Web, an excellent way to browse is to use either a combination search tool/subject directory such as Yahoo! or a discipline-based subject directory such as the World Wide Web Virtual Library.

6f Note-Taking Strategies

Develop an effective method for note taking. Some writers use research notebooks that are divided into several sections: one for logging research activities, one for taking notes, one for working up a bibliography, and one for idea generating and writing rough drafts. Other writers use note cards for both notes and bibliographic information. You can adapt either the notebook or the note-card technique to your own needs, combining traditional note cards and notebooks with their electronic equivalents.

Note-taking skills take time to develop. Follow the techniques listed below, and adapt them to your needs:

- Keep a careful record of every source that is even remotely promising. References that seem only tangentially related to your topic early in the research process may prove crucial in the future. You will have less trouble locating the source later if you have accurate bibliographic information.
- Evaluate your sources critically. Do not take notes on a source unless you are fairly certain that it contains the kind of information you need. See pages 41–42 and Checklist 7 for evaluation guidelines.
- Keep note cards separate from bibliography cards so that you can sort notes without disturbing the bibliography-cards file. Include sufficient information to link the note card with the more complete bibliography card. You may be accustomed to using note cards only to paraphrase, summarize, or record quotes from such sources as books and journal articles. You can, however, also use note cards to summarize interviews with experts and to jot down your own ideas and insights.
- Poor note taking can result in errors in your quotes and citations, possibly leaving you open to plagiarism. (See section 9e, "Avoiding Plagiarism," pages 49–50.) If you prepare sum-

maries and paraphrases while reading your sources, be careful to indicate with quotation marks the exact words used in the source. To ensure that you are truly paraphrasing, try writing down the author's ideas without the source open in front of you.

ONLINE TIP ▸ Electronic Note and Bibliography Cards

1. Create a template file for each master card. Customize the cards as needed to accommodate your sources. Since the cards are designed for a word processor, the space will expand as needed.

Note Card

> Key words:
> Author or brief title:
> Notes:
> Personal response to this source:

Bibliography Card

> Author(s)/editor(s):
> Title:
> Volume:
> City/publisher:
> Date of publication:
> Value of this source:

2. After you design the cards, use the Cut and Paste functions of your word processor to make multiple copies of the text in the file.
3. Each time you use the file, save a copy of it with a new name so that you can use your original template (bibliography-card file or note-card file) for another project.
4. Head each note card with a key word or words that represent(s) an important concept in the source. You can then search your file to find all the notes you have taken on a specific topic with the same key words. For example, if you are writing about problems in the legal system and want to find all of the notes you have taken that include the key words *defense attorneys*, search for all instances of *defense*. By searching a file that contains all your notes, you will be able to find and reorganize your notes by copying all related items to a new file.
5. When you take notes, indicate the usefulness or value of each source in a section of your bibliography card; also indicate your personal reaction to the source on your note card.

7 Evaluating Your Sources

You need to have a good command of your subject in order to spot biases and information gaps. Until you are well acquainted with your topic, you will not be in a good position to evaluate sources fairly. Thus you should do considerable background reading before conducting a thorough evaluation of your sources.

Evaluating Sources

CHECKLIST 7

- Is the source appropriate for your topic? Do you need a scholarly source rather than a popular magazine article? Do you need a book on the topic rather than a synopsis on a Website?
- Is the source reputable? Is it a well-respected publishing company, a university press, a refereed journal, or a well-established Website?
- Is the author an authority on the topic? Don't assume that just because an author is recognized as an expert in the field, every book he or she writes is equally good. Examine the author's argument and the evidence.
- Is the author's argument for a given point well supported? Note whether the author appears to be distorting facts in order to support his or her own theory.
- Does the author present only one side of an argument? If so, does the author acknowledge that there are opposing viewpoints?
- Does the source have a particular point of view or bias? Is the author conscious of this bias? (Everyone sees the world differently, thus all sources have some kind of bias. A fair-minded author will make this bias apparent to readers.)

ADDITIONAL WEB-PAGE CONSIDERATIONS

- Who is the sponsor of the site? Who updates the site—a service provider, a university, a business, an activist group? Who posts to the site—experts, students, the general public? One way to check is to click on a home page, if available, and read the author's resume.
- Is the site the best place to find information on this topic, or would a journal article or book be more appropriate?
- Do all the sites on your list present similar views of the topic? Some topics on the Web, such as censorship, tend to reflect similar views. You must intentionally look for sites that represent different points of view.
- Is the site current? Many good sites have not been kept up to date by their authors.

Many less-than-reputable books can appear on library shelves. Similarly, many magazines include articles written by nonspecialists and should be quoted only if they truly fit the nature of your paper. And all texts have biases that need to be examined critically so that you are aware of the authors' perspectives. Finally, because of the democratic nature of the Internet, Web sources are especially problematic, for anyone who has access to a Web server can publish anything he or she chooses.

If your topic is a scholarly one, then you should try to locate scholarly sources (refereed journals and books from university presses). If your topic is a popular one—for example, financing a home purchase, or caring for dogs, or intellectual-property debates on the Web, or even censorship issues—you can use carefully selected Web sources.

All sources (books, magazines and journals, newspapers, and the Web) should be scrutinized to determine whether they are appropriate for your research paper. Do not cite a source merely because it is authoritative; rather, cite valid sources that provide a reader with background information on your topic or that provide evidence for your main ideas. Even if you have taken the time to read a book in its entirety, one that has been highly acclaimed, you should not quote it in your paper if it does not provide useful insights into your topic. Part of evaluating sources involves examining their usefulness for your research.

8 Writing the Research Paper

In reality, you start writing a research paper from the moment you begin considering topics and doing background reading and note taking. Writing refers to much more than getting the words in the right order and designing unified paragraphs, regardless of whether the goal is a short essay or a longer, documented paper. Recognizing the unique nature of a research paper can help you develop strategies and processes that are appropriate to the task at hand.

Organization is especially important for research tasks, where you have many bits and pieces of information to consider. If you have kept your notes in a separate file and saved the file with a new name, you can write your draft in the same file you used for note taking. Or you could work with your note files in one window, your draft file in another.

8a Developing a Controlling Idea

Review your notes regularly with the aim of discovering a focus for your paper. (You may also want to refer to section 4, "Framing the Main Ideas," pages 18–22.) Your sources will often direct you toward a focus. For instance, while preparing to write a paper on Web censorship, you may find that your sources challenge your earlier thinking and move you toward a different focus than the one you had when you began.

Eventually, you will be able to narrow your focus still further and explore one aspect of your topic in greater depth. The sample paper on pages 51–54, for example, considers one aspect of the censorship issue: the problem of finding software that effectively blocks indecent sites from students. If your paper will be longer than three or four pages, plan to do some preliminary organizing before you begin drafting, and refer to section 2d, "An Exploratory Draft" (page 13).

8b Drafting the Paper

When you are ready to draft, give yourself the time to write for a few days or weeks. Divide your topic into several parts, label each part, and work on each separately. Explore different ways of using the power of your word processor to assist you as you compose. For example, consider creating a folder for your research paper and subfolders for different components of the paper. If you want, you can store notes for each section of your paper in a different subfolder.

As you draft different sections of your paper, you may discover that you need more information. Only when you draft your essay can you determine what additional information you

Drafting a Research Paper ONLINE TIP

1. Use the outline template suggested on page 17 to create your draft; then move notes from your electronic note cards to appropriate places in this draft file.
2. Use one window for trying out versions of sentences and paragraphs. Then Copy and Paste them into a second window that you are using for your draft.
3. If your word processor has an outline view, move between outline and normal view as you work.

may need. As you draft one section of your paper, you may think of ideas that you could use in another section. Jot down your ideas, then move them to the end of your file. Either keep them at the end of the file or transfer them to your research notebook.

8c Revising Your Work

When you have finished drafting your entire paper, take time to revise it, referring to section 5, "Revising" (pages 22–28). Many students find that after they have written their drafts, they must rearrange the material so that the paper says what they want it to say, eliminate points that aren't developed, or gather more information to support what they have said. One technique that can help is the descriptive outline. A descriptive outline is done after you write a draft. In your outline, you write labels on your draft that describe not what you wanted to say in each section, but what you actually have said. When you are finished, you should be able to look more critically at your paper and make your revisions. Remember to save a copy of your file with a new name before you write descriptive headings in it.

9 Using Sources in Your Paper

Your finished research paper should reflect your ability to weave quotations and references into your own text. As you draft, indicate the source of your information, or, at the very least, note the name and page numbers of your sources; when you edit your finished draft, carefully revise each citation so that it conforms to one of the standard documentation systems. (See the sample research paper on pages 51–54.)

9a Documentation Systems

Documentation systems are standard ways that writers in a given field credit their sources by citing them in the text and listing them in a bibliography at the end of the paper. Undergraduates are most commonly asked to use either of two documentation systems: the Modern Language Association's (MLA) or the American Psychological Association's (APA). Both these systems use what is called parenthetical citation—that is, references to sources are placed in parentheses in the sentences themselves. Footnotes are reserved for explanatory notes or comments and are used only when an explanation cannot be incorporated into the text.

The bibliography or list of sources is referred to as Works Cited in MLA style and as References in APA style. In both cases,

---

Sources That Must Be Cited

CHECKLIST 8

DIRECT QUOTATIONS
Quote directly from your source if the original words are unique and distinctive or if they add authority to your point. At times, you may decide to include a direct quotation simply because the content of the original passage cannot be paraphrased without destroying the impact of the author's words.

IDEAS THAT ARE SUMMARIZED OR PARAPHRASED
Paraphasing or summarizing a source is often preferable to quoting, for it allows you as the author to use your own style and voice in your research paper. Always remember to use parenthetical citations for such sources, just as you would if you were quoting them.

IDEAS AND OPINIONS ASSOCIATED WITH A PARTICULAR PERSON
If you refer to specific concepts adhered to by one economist, such as John Maynard Keynes, you must include a reference to him. Otherwise, a reader might assume that you had created that economic theory yourself.

DATA THAT, IN THE CONTEXT OF YOUR PAPER, MAY BE OPEN TO DISPUTE
If you cite statistics related to smoking among college students, you need to include a reference to your source.

COMPILATION OF INFORMATION IN GRAPHS, TABLES, AND CHARTS
If you use information from a table or a chart, you need to cite it, even if you do not reproduce the chart in your paper.

RESULTS OF SURVEYS YOU HAVE CONDUCTED AS PART OF YOUR RESEARCH
You should include the survey instrument itself in an Appendix.

QUOTATIONS OR SUMMARIES FROM INTERVIEWS
If interviews are personal, you can call them "personal communication" in your bibliography.

this list should contain only those sources that you either quote, summarize, or paraphrase.

In these citation styles, when you refer to the author and/or the work in your sentence, do not repeat that information in the parenthetical citation. The purpose of a parenthetical citation is to to direct the reader to the complete citation at the end of your paper—it is a shorthand. (For more on in-text citation, see pages 47–49.)

9b What to Cite

As you write, cite all information that is not commonly known about your topic. You must acknowledge (by placing within quotation marks) the exact words taken from another source, including any distinctive individual word or short phrase, and all individual sentences or strung-together phrases. You must also acknowledge the source of material you paraphrase: any distinctive ideas that you found elsewhere and are restating in your own words.

Exactly what to document will vary according to what information and expectations you can assume your readers have about the subject as well as what you have given your audience in your text.

9c Paraphrasing, Summarizing, and Quoting

Let your thesis provide the momentum of ideas in your research paper. Use paraphrases, summaries, and quotations to support what you want to say. As much as possible, write paraphrases and summaries of your sources on your note cards, rather than using direct quotations. You will, however, want to record some quotations—especially if they express an idea succinctly—even if you are not sure that you will use them.

PARAPHRASING   A paraphrase is a restatement of a portion of text in your own words. The paraphrased text should follow the gist of the original source and should be roughly the same length.

ORIGINAL   In a 7–2 decision, the Supreme Court struck down the Communications Decency Act, a law that made it a crime to make "indecent" or "patently offensive" material available to minors over the fast-growing Internet and other computer networks.

PARAPHRASE   The Supreme Court, by a margin of 7 to 2,
overturned the CDA, an attempt to control the kind
of material that could be disseminated to minors on
the Internet (Schwartz and Biskupic A1+).

SUMMARIZING   A **summary** is a condensed version of a text
of any length and should be much shorter than the original
text. The following sentence summarizes a five-page article:

▶ According to a Website entitled "A Dozen Reasons Why
Schools Should Avoid Filtering," within fourteen minutes an
experienced Internet user can find many sites with pornographic
content.

Note: Because there is no author for this reference and the one
that follows, no parenthetical citation is needed at the end of
the sentence. The Works Cited provides the full reference.

QUOTING   Use direct quotations sparingly, quoting only sentences that express the idea in ways that could not be well represented in a paraphrase or a summary. Direct quotations must
contain the exact words of your source.

▶ As a Website on surf-patrol programs notes, "Even though
cybersnoopers often employ knowbots and spiders to dig up
and then filter any site which includes the use of various words
such as sex and naked, the enemy is also clever, changing its
spelling to baffle and confound the electronic hounds" ("Dozen
Reasons" 1).

9d Incorporating Source Information into Sentences

Introduce source information into your sentences naturally.
Parenthetical citations should provide readers with an immediate sense of how much of a text is your own and how much
is based on other writers' work. Even though these citations do
not provide comprehensive information, they should give readers enough data about the author and the title of the source to
reduce the need to consult continually separate endnotes or to
turn to the Works Cited page.

Place citations carefully to keep your own text uncluttered.
Parenthetical citations are best placed at a natural pause in the
sentence, preferably at the end. Provide as much information
as possible in the text itself.

Below are some suggestions for varying the style in which you incorporate paraphrases, summaries, and quotations:

1. Use tag words such as "according to" or "as the author notes" to introduce the portion of the quotation you want to cite.

   ▶ According to the *Washington Post*, "civil libertarians and businesses hoping to profit from the Internet were elated by the strongly worded decision" (Schwartz and Biskupic 17).

2. Incorporate only a phrase or a few words from the original.

   ▶ Justice John Paul Stevens understood that the Communications Decency Act would have threatened "to torch a large segment of the Internet community" (qtd. in Schwartz and Biskupic 17).

   Note: Often you will find one author quoted in another author's text. The above parenthetical citation is correct for this kind of situation. (See page 60 for more information.)

3. Use ellipsis points (. . .) to eliminate irrelevant material from a quotation and brackets [ ] to clarify any words in the original or to make your sentence clearer. If the ellipsis occurs at the end of a sentence, you need to add a period.

   ▶ Justice John Paul Stevens explained that current cases "provide no basis for qualifying the level of . . . scrutiny that should be applied. . . ." He continued by noting that "the law [the CDA] threatens to torch a large segment of the Internet community" (qtd. in Schwartz and Biskupic 17).

4. Incorporate portions of direct quotations into a paraphrase.

   ▶ Justice Stevens found that the CDA was too vague to enforce and noted that he saw no reason for "scrutinizing" speech on the Internet in an intrusive way, for by attempting to protect the rights of children, this kind of law could "torch . . . the Internet" (qtd. in Schwartz and Biskupic 17).

1. Open your note files in one or more windows and your document file in another so that you can Copy and Paste any notes or drafts from your note or draft files into your document.
2. Integrate your notes into your paragraphs. You will probably have to make major revisions, including changing from direct quotes to paraphrases or summaries, depending on the context in which they appear in your paper.
3. Always mention the source (either by title or by description) and the page number of the source in your draft—for example, "(*Washington Post* story, page 1)." You can revise for proper documentation style later.

9e Avoiding Plagiarism

The act of passing off the words or ideas of another as one's own is called **plagiarism**. The work you improperly pass off as your own can be that of a published author or of a classmate and, in both cases, either the actual words used by that person or that person's distinctive ideas. In all colleges and universities, plagiarism is a serious violation of academic ethics and is grounds for severe penalty.

Dealing with summaries and paraphrases always remains a potential source of difficulty for student writers. (See section 9c, "Paraphrasing, Summarizing, and Quoting," pages 46–47.) Sometimes students will prepare paraphrases and summaries that very closely follow parts of the original source, including some direct quotations, but will neglect to add the quotation marks; then weeks later, when they compose their paper, they may forget just which words and phrases are their own and which come directly from the original source. Remember that when you take notes, you must put quotation marks around all direct quotations; and, to be certain that paraphrases and summaries are truly in your own words, you should write them without looking at the original sources.

Dealing with distinctive ideas is not as precise as dealing with exact words, and here a few guidelines are in order. It is often to your rhetorical advantage as a would-be expert to attribute specific ideas to specific people; one sign of being an expert yourself is knowing which other experts to cite. Within a normal class discussion, many ideas will be exchanged. Here, too, it is both ethically required and a sign of strong writing that you acknowledge in your text specific classmates as the source of specific insights. This is especially necessary if your class is using online workshopping and the regular sharing of papers—a situation that will also allow you to quote directly from classmates, an acceptable practice as long as you use quotation marks and acknowledge the source in your text. You might also want to cite your professors in your text. Check with your individual professors as to whether or not you should cite them as sources for ideas that they raise during normal class discussion. Your professors may possibly expect you to consider these ideas as belonging to the public domain of the class, in which case you could cite them without attribution.

When you cite Internet sources, be sure to give credit, using the appropriate citation format (see pages 63 and 71–73). Respect the "intellectual property" of Internet authors: cite anonymous as well as authored sources. In addition, it is considered good etiquette to write to the author of an E-mail, newsgroup, or Listserv message, requesting permission to cite him or her in your paper.

Remember the general rule to cite all sources of distinctive or controversial information and to use direct quotations when citing other people's exact words, whether published or not. Finally, as a matter of style, try to resist the temptation to quote others extensively.

9f Moving Beyond Print Research Papers

Many word processors today allow you to make links within your document to Web sources that supplement or clarify your points. By underlining a key word, selecting the link icon from the menu bar, and inserting the Web address, you can create hyperlinks to Web information. For example, in the paper on censorship at the end of this chapter, the writer could link to the full text of the Communications Decency Act or to the articles referred to in the Works Cited. Then, when the paper is read at a computer connected to the World Wide Web, readers can click on the underlined words to read the supplementary information, if they wish.

You may want to publish your writing on your own home page, or your teacher may have created a Website for your class. By saving your paper in **HTML** (Hypertext Markup Language) **format**, the format used on the World Wide Web, you can prepare your work for Web publication. As your skill in using the Web develops, you may begin to create complex research projects, with audio, sound, and text images and hyperlinked pages.

10 Sample Research Paper Using MLA Parenthetical Style

Joel Martinez
Ms. Lee
EH 309-002
16 July 1998

An Alternative to Cyber-Patrol Software

Everyone has read horror stories about the abundance of pornography on the Internet and the growing number of stalkers who cruise the Internet looking for easy prey (Gill 176; Gilbert). But just how much of a problem is there? Many school districts across the country have assumed there will be problems. Rather than help their teachers prepare for possibilities, schools have installed "cyber patrol" programs that block access to Websites that may contain sensitive material. A more effective solution is for schools to encourage students to develop a sense of self-discipline and to help them learn how to select or reject materials themselves.

The Supreme Court struck down the Censorship Decency Act (CDA), which would have blocked indecent material for the schools. The authors of CDA had proposed a legal way of controlling the exchange of what they referred to as "indecent" material on the Internet (Stecher). Responding to the fears of parents and special interest groups, they designed a bill that would have changed the nature of the Internet. They thought that the Internet was more like television or radio than like print and assumed that so-called "service providers," the companies that offer Internet services, could be responsible for the content of information on their sites. Contesting the bill on the basis that it violated the First Amendment, the ACLU maintained that the CDA would, in effect, limit the kinds of private messages that people would be willing to trust sending to each other on such topics as abortion and AIDS ("US Judges").

Internet fans were encouraged by the justices' decision. The justices clearly had begun to understand the way the Internet works. Justice John Paul Stevens understood that the Communications Decency Act would have threatened "to torch a large segment of the Internet community" (qtd. in Schwartz and Biskupic 17). He and the other justices recognized that the problems censorship would cause are worse than the potential benefits.

Unfortunately, the Supreme Court didn't offer solutions to the smut overflow on the Web. Without knowing what to do, schools and parents turned to apparent solutions—cyber-patrol software that can be installed on home and school computers, and ratings systems that alert viewers to the nature of sites they are about to see. Ultimately, these solutions are inappropriate. Cyber-patrol software is unreliable, and questionable sites are not likely to use rating systems. The best solution is the one that puts the responsibility for viewing into the hands of the individual—either child, teacher, or parent.

So-called surf-patrol programs claim to be foolproof but are not at all reliable. According to the authors of "A Dozen Reasons Why Schools Should Avoid Filtering," within fourteen minutes they were able to find many sites with pornographic content. For "even though cybersnoopers often employ knowbots and spiders to dig up and then filter any site which includes the use of various words such as sex and naked, the enemy is also clever, changing its spelling to baffle and confound the electronic hounds" (1).

Clearly, cyber-patrol programs don't block all indecent sites. As one example of the cleverness of "the enemy," let me offer a personal example. A surf-patrol program wouldn't have blocked out the sight I found last year as I searched for information about the Heavensgate cult for a college research paper. Here's what happened. I searched for "heavensgate" using InfoSeek. Next, I clicked on the top-ranked "hit" from InfoSeek, which welcomed all those interested in the Heavensgate incident. Jake's porno shop appeared on the screen. I exited right away and figured out how this had happened. The word "heavensgate" was repeated about two hundred times in the abstract that the site developers submitted to InfoSeek and to other search engines. Lesson learned: read the abstract before clicking on the results of a search!

Nor do cyber-patrol programs give students and teachers open access to material they may want for justifiable purposes. For example, a teacher in my hometown has told me that she couldn't even retrieve Shakespeare's plays. The program used in her district, Net Nanny, blocked any sites that use sexually explicit terms (Moreno).

The judges who wrote the Communications Decency Act had a sincere interest in protecting children from the dangers of the Internet. They felt that the law, which carried fines up to $250,000 and prison terms of up to five years, would protect children from pornography. Unfortunately, the kind of censorship that the CDA advocated would have had too many negative effects to make it worthwhile. Because the judges didn't suggest a solution to the censorship problem, schools and families and individuals continue to grapple with the issue, offering useless solutions that attempt to take the responsibility for blocking indecent or pornographic sites away from the individual viewer.

The only sensible, long-term solution is self-discipline. It is essential that people develop their own inner sense of what is decent and what isn't. It is also critical that teachers and parents help children develop the skills needed to safely navigate the Internet. As more and more people understand the Internet and learn how to use it responsibly, it is less and less likely that the government will be called on again to legislate decency.

It is not going to be easy for teachers or parents to figure out ways to teach self-discipline and at the same time teach students how to search effectively. After all, if students learn how to search effectively, they will be able to locate any material they want. That is where the self-discipline comes in. If students develop a sense of the value of the Internet for democracy, they may willingly impose some discipline on themselves. A Website called "Legal Pad Junior" is one example of the kind of Internet development that would help teachers and parents help young people. This Internet site focuses on introducing young people to the legal field. It is, however, also fun to use, and it encourages children to see themselves as equal partners with adults on the Web. The site contains a legal directory, hints for Internet users, a "Kidz Zone," a "Teenz Connection," a place called the "Clubhouse," and an area called "i-SAFE Connection," which invites students to join discussions of Internet safety.

It is essential that children learn how the Internet has developed and how to use it effectively for information gathering. It is also important that children learn how to avoid unsafe Internet sites and how to protect themselves if they stumble on them or if they are approached by unsavory individuals. As the "Charter of Children's Rights in Telematic Networks" proclaims: "A child who has not been given the opportunity to learn how to manage the world of tomorrow . . . will have minor chances of success."

Martinez

Works Cited

"A Charter of Children's Rights in Telematic Networks." Sept. 1996. 10 Dec. 1997. ⟨http://www.efa.org.au/Issues/Censor/cens2.html⟩.

"A Dozen Reasons Why Schools Should Avoid Filtering." From Now On: The Educational Technology Journal 5.5 (1996): 1‑5. 10 Nov. 1997. ⟨http://fromnowon.org/Mar96/whynot.html⟩.

Gilbert, Steven. "Welcome to the Internet: Nightmare or Paradise?" American Association of Higher Education Bulletin 46.7 (1994): 3-4.

Gill, Mark Stuart. "Terror On-Line." Vogue Jan. 1995: 163-67+.

"Legal Pad Junior." 10 Dec. 1997. ⟨http://www.legalpadjr.com/⟩.

Moreno, Dan. Personal communication. 10 Nov. 1997.

Schwartz, John, and Joan Biskupic. "High Court Allows Bans on Assisted Suicide, Strikes down Law Restricting Online Speech: First Amendment Applies to Internet, Justices Say. Washington Post 27 July 1997: A1+.

Stecher, Jamie B. "ACLU v. Reno--the Case to Overturn the CDA." Ethical Spectacle (19 Feb. 1997). 8 Nov. 1997. ⟨http://www.spectacle.org/cda/cdamn.html⟩.

"US Judges Declare Internet Decency Law Unconstitutional." Nando Times (29 July 1996). 10 Nov. 1997. ⟨http://www.nando.net/newsroom/ntm/info/072996/info25_6695.html⟩.

Documentation

In all academic writing, you must acknowledge sources of information, ideas, or words. This book considers several documentation systems: the Modern Language Association (MLA) and the American Psychological Association (APA) styles are described in detail; the Council of Biology Editors (CBE) and the Turabian styles are discussed briefly.

11 MLA Documentation

MLA style consists of parenthetical references to sources you have consulted. In parentheses, you indicate the author and page reference of the source you have used at that point in your paper. To locate the complete source, the reader refers to the list of works cited (Works Cited) at the end of the paper. Footnotes or endnotes can be used sparingly to provide supplementary information to readers.

11a In-Text Citation Format

MLA citation requires two pieces of information, either in your text or in parentheses:

1. The name of the source, usually indicated by the name(s) of the author(s).
2. The page reference(s) in that source. If you are citing the entire source, you can omit the page reference(s).

These citations are referred to as either ''in-text'' or parenthetical citations.

Your citation must include specific portions of the reference information listed in the Works Cited. How much you include in your in-text citation depends on the information you present in your text. If you do not mention the author in your sentence, you need to note the author's name and the page number in parentheses in your text. If you mention the author, you need only put the page number in parentheses at the end of the sentence. If there is no author, use key words from the title to indicate your source. Note how the citation and the corresponding Works Cited entry complement one another.

▶ In a recent editorial in the *Valley Morning Star*, a graduate discussed problems he had had in getting accepted to several institutions without Affirmative Action programs ("Importance" A1).

Works Cited

"The Importance of Affirmative Action." Editorial. *Valley Morning Star* 14 Sept. 1997: A1–3.

If the name of the author of your source is clear from your text, it should not be repeated in the parenthetical citation.

▶ Cinque, the main character in Alex Pate's *Amistad*, recognizes that "it was he who would have to lead" the rebellion (19).

The page number(s) can be omitted for a one-page article or for a reference source arranged alphabetically.

▶ *Eulogy*, as defined by the *Harper Handbook to Literature*, is "a speech or composition of praise, especially of a deceased person."

ONE WORK BY ONE AUTHOR If the author's name is not referred to in your sentence, include the last name and the page number in parentheses. There is no comma between the author and the page number.

▶ Although computers may lead to many improvements in education, critics contend that computers lack the ability to provide a "cure for ills that are social and political in nature" (Roszak 219).

▶ Although computers may lead to many improvements in education, computer critic Theodore Roszak contends that they lack the ability to provide a "cure for ills that are social and political in nature" (219).

► The advent of printing, writes historian Elizabeth Eisenstein, is of such importance because it led to "fundamental alterations in prevailing patterns of continuity and change" (2: 703).

Note: In a multivolume work, use a colon to separate the volume and page numbers: "(Eisenstein 2: 703)."

TWO OR MORE WORKS BY ONE AUTHOR If you will be citing more than one work by an author, include a short form of the title (usually the first one or two words, excluding *a, an,* and *the*). If you mention the author in your text, then the title of the work and the page reference (unless you are referring to the entire book) are all you need.

► As a hopeful symbol of the modern age, the personal computer "supplies answers and restores composure" (McCorduck, *Universal* 284). The prospects for artificial intelligence, McCorduck concludes in an earlier work, are "nearly beyond comprehension" (*Machines* 357).

The complete title for the first reference is *The Universal Machine*; for the second reference, it is *Machines Who Think*. Remember to be consistent in your use of the abbreviated form of the author's work.

ONE WORK WITH TWO OR MORE AUTHORS With two or three authors, include the last name of each author either in your text or in parentheses.

► Teachers have to be trained in the use of technology (Brooke, Levin, and Stanley 199).

With more than three authors, include the last name of the first author listed plus "et al." (an abbreviation of *et alii*, "and others").

► In revising an essay, writing experts contend, it is important to "attend to the major problems first" (Lauer et al. 284).

WORK WITH AN AUTHOR AND EDITOR Some collections of texts include an editor who has assembled the collection and who may have written an introduction or a preface, and one or more authors whose work is included in the collection. Clarify in your text (and enter accordingly in your Works Cited) the person—editor or author—to whom you are referring.

► Culture allows us to reconsider with a critical eye what Victorian critic Matthew Arnold refers to as "our stock notions and habits" (6).

▶ In J. Dover Wilson's words, Arnold "shuddered" (xviii) at the lack of culture in nineteenth-century England.

CORPORATE AUTHOR   Cite a corporate author by its full corporate name, including, where possible, that name in your text as introductory material or, as a parenthetical insertion, at the end of your sentence.

▶ In his hearing before the United States Atomic Energy Commission, J. Robert Oppenheimer expressed "grave concern and anxiety" about the development of the hydrogen bomb (229).

▶ In his hearing to regain his security clearance, J. Robert Oppenheimer stated that the development of the hydrogen bomb was a matter of "grave concern and anxiety" (United States Atomic Energy Commission 229).

NO AUTHOR OR ANONYMOUS   Identify works without authors by title, using only the first word or words of a long title.

▶ Fortunately, an article in the *New Republic* criticized early proposals that only native-born Americans be allowed to withdraw foreign language books from libraries ("American" A106).

AUTHOR QUOTED BY ANOTHER SOURCE   Include "qtd. in" ("quoted in") before the name of your source.

▶ Sir Bernard Lovely notes that overly narrow and regimented computerized research in astronomy is damaging to "the free exercise of that happy faculty known as serendipity" (qtd. in Roszak 115).

AUTHORS WITH THE SAME NAME   If a paper includes references to different works by authors who have the same last name, refer in your text to the first instance of the reference by using the author's complete first name and last name.

▶ In her article on computers in composition classes, Dawn Rodrigues notes that teachers should combine instruction in word processing with instruction in composition (3–4). In his article on teacher evaluation, Raymond Rodrigues stresses the importance of explaining teaching techniques to administrators (88–89).

If your in-text citation is fully parenthetical, however, you must add the first initial to the author's last name.

▶ An article on computers and composition classes notes that teachers should combine instruction in word processing with instruction in composition (D. Rodrigues 3–4). In another article on teacher evaluation, the importance of explaining teaching techniques to administrators is stressed (R. Rodrigues 88–89).

TWO OR MORE WORKS IN ONE CITATION Give the parenthetical citations to two or more sources as you normally would, separating the citations with semicolons.

By different authors

▶ Both agree that electronic mail is important (Hawisher and LeBlanc 3; Eldred 47).

The above example assumes that only one work by each author is included in the paper.

▶ Both agree that electronic mail is important (Hawisher and LeBlanc, *Electronic* 3; Eldred, *Mediating* 47).

This example assumes that the Works Cited includes more than one reference by each author.

By the same author

▶ The influence of computers on society is noted frequently in discussions of computers in instruction in writing (Selfe, *Situating*; Selfe, *Designing*).

This example assumes that entire works by one author are being referred to—hence, the shortened titles and no page references.

PART OF A SOURCE Include the page number and, when it does not appear in the text, the author's last name when referring to a specific part of a work.

▶ Although computers may lead to many improvements in education, critics contend that computers lack the ability to provide a "cure for ills that are social and political in nature" (Roszak 219).

PERSONAL COMMUNICATION Since readers will find it difficult to check the information contained in a personal communication, try to cite such references in the text. (Remember to list such references in the Works Cited.)

▶ According to John M. Thomas (letter to the author), our company will adopt flex-time work policies this summer.

LITERATURE   When citing a classical play, omit the page reference, and cite by section (act, scene) and line number, using either Arabic numbers or Roman numerals or a combination of both.

▶ In Shakespeare's *Hamlet*, Polonius advises Laertes to "give thy thoughts no tongue" (1.3.59).

▶ In Shakespeare's *Hamlet*, Polonius advises Laertes to "give thy thoughts no tongue" (I.iii.59).

Do not cite poetry by page. Instead, cite by section number (if appropriate) and line number or, for poems without numbered lines, by title.

▶ In "Song of Myself," Whitman identifies himself with the "procreant urge of the world" (line 45).

For the last citation, use the word *line* or *lines* to prevent your reader from confusing *l.* and *ll.* with the numbers one and eleven. Once it is established that the numbers refer to lines and not pages, you can then cite the numbers alone.

THE BIBLE   To cite a book of the Bible, do not underline it or use quotation marks around it; follow it with the chapter and verse numbers.

▶ (Genesis 39.23)

Note: Ordinarily, you would include the Bible only in your in-text citation, not in your Works Cited.

NONPRINT SOURCES SUCH AS FILMS AND RECORDINGS   In your text, cite the title and/or the name of the person chiefly responsible for that work, and enter the complete reference to that work under the person's name in your Works Cited.

▶ Cinematographer Nestor Almendros does some of his finest work in capturing the rural Texas landscapes in *Places in the Heart*.

ELECTRONIC SOURCES   When you refer to electronic sources such as Websites, online databases, E-mail communications, and electronic journals, follow the same guidelines you use for citing print sources: either refer to the author and page number (if available) in the text itself or in parentheses at the end of the sentence. Electronic sources frequently are not paginated, however. You have the choice of referring to the paragraph number, indicating that there are no pages, or simply not including any reference to page numbers or paragraphs. (Don't confuse the page numbers that appear when you print Web sources with actual page numbers. The pages that emerge from your printer are numbered by the software on your computer and vary in length, depending on the size you specify in your page setup program.) Again, as with print sources, if the citation has no author, then refer to the title both in your textual citation and in the Works Cited.

> ▶ The University of Hawaii's Center for Hawaiian Studies has developed a Website that provides information about the country's history and its native people ("Hawaiian Language Center").

> ▶ In "English Only," a World Wide Web briefing paper on the English Only movement, the American Civil Liberties Union maintains that English Only laws are founded on "false stereotypes of immigrant groups."

In the above example, there is no in-text citation because the corporate author of the site—the American Civil Liberties Union—as well as the title of the Web source ("English Only") are referred to in the sentence. The Works Cited entry would appear as follows:

American Civil Liberties Union. "English Only." 7 July 1997. ⟨http://www.aclu.org/library/pbp6.html⟩.

11b Works Cited

Starting on a new page entitled "Works Cited" and using the MLA style, list all the works you have cited—and only those you have cited. Treat each entry separately, putting the first line of each entry flush against the left margin and indenting all subsequent lines of that entry approximately five characters or one-half inch from the left margin.

Arrange entries alphabetically by the author's last name or, when you have no author's name, by the first significant word in the title. When you have several works by the same author, list the entries alphabetically by title. Give the author's name in the first entry only; thereafter, use three hyphens followed by a period and a space in place of the author's name.

ONLINE TIP ▸ Bibliographic Tools

If you have access to bibliography software, explore its usefulness to you. There are two kinds of software tools that can help you prepare a bibliography:

1. **FORMATTING TOOLS**   Some programs ask you to enter each piece of information as a field in a database and then automatically display this information for you in MLA or APA format. The tricky part of such helpful programs is making certain that the data get printed correctly as part of your paper—with proper page number, header, and font.

2. **BIBLIOGRAPHIC GUIDELINE PROGRAMS**   Some programs provide an online guide to bibliographic format. As you type your entries, either as word processing text or in a separate part of the word processing program, this kind of program will automatically alphabetize entries and format them with the proper indention.

11c Works Cited Entries: Books

The main divisions for each book entry are as follows:

1. **Author**   Give the author's last name first, followed by a comma, then the first name, and a period.
2. **Title**   State the book's full title, separating the subtitle from the title with a colon. Italicize (underline) the full title, and place a period at the end.
3. **Publication Information**   Include the *place of publication*, the *publisher*, and the *date of publication*.
   - If more than one city of publication is mentioned, give the first city of publication only.
   - Shorten names of well-known publishers, omitting articles ("A," "And," "The") but keeping "UP" for "University Press" ("Norton," rather than "W. W. Norton & Company"; "Iowa UP," rather than "Iowa University Press").
   - Use the latest copyright date if no date is given on the title page or "n.d." if no date is given at all.

The following are variations and/or examples of MLA bibliographic style for citing books.

BOOK WITH ONE AUTHOR AND/OR EDITOR

McDonald, Frances Beck. *Censorship and Intellectual Freedom.* Metuchen, NJ: Scarecrow, 1993.

Tompkins, Jane, ed. *Reader-Response Criticism: From Formalism to Structuralism.* Baltimore: Johns Hopkins UP, 1980.

BOOK WITH AN EDITOR'S MATERIAL Referring to the editor's material only:

Wilson, J. Dover, ed. Introduction. *Culture and Anarchy.* By Matthew Arnold. New York: Cambridge UP, 1961.

Using a cross reference to refer to both editor and author:

Wilson, J. Dover. Introduction. Arnold xi–xl.

SECOND OR LATER EDITION OF A BOOK

Lauer, Janice, et al. *Four Worlds of Writing.* 2nd ed. New York: Harper, 1985.

Note: Other abbreviations commonly used for second or later editions are "rev." for "revised," "enl." for "enlarged," and "abr." for "abridged."

BOOK WITH TWO OR THREE AUTHORS OR EDITORS

Crawford, John C., and Dorothy L. Crawford. *Expressionism and Twentieth-Century Music.* Bloomington: Indiana UP, 1993.

Use the order of the names given on the title page, inverting only the first name.

BOOK WITH FOUR OR MORE AUTHORS

Lauer, Janice, et al. *Four Worlds of Writing.* 2nd ed. New York: Harper, 1985.

Give the name of the first author listed on the title page, and add "et al.," which stands for *et alii* (Latin for "and others").

BOOK OF TWO OR MORE VOLUMES

Eisenstein, Elizabeth L. *The Printing Press as an Agent of Change*. 2 vols. New York: Cambridge UP, 1979.

BOOK IN A NUMBERED SERIES

Wolf, Maryanne, Mark K. McQuillan, and Eugene Radwin. *Thought and Language/Language and Reading*. Reprint Ser. 14. Cambridge: Harvard Educational Review, 1980.

REPRINT OF A BOOK

Huey, Edmund Burke. *The Psychology and Pedagogy of Reading*. 1908. Cambridge: MIT P, 1968.

BOOK IN TRANSLATION

Kristeva, Julia. *In the Beginning Was Love: Psychoanalysis and Faith*. Trans. Rosemary Edmonds. New York: Columbia UP, 1987.

Begin the entry with the translator's name if you wish to cite the translator's introduction or notes.

Edmonds, Rosemary, trans. *Fathers and Sons*. By Ivan Turgenev. 1861. New York: Penguin, 1965. vi–xix.

BOOK WITH AN ANONYMOUS AUTHOR

Peterson's Competitive Colleges, 1998–99. Princeton: Peterson's Guides, 1998.

IMPRINT

Orwell, George. *1984*. 1949. New York: Signet Classic–NAL, 1961.

BOOK PUBLISHED BEFORE 1900

Dewey, John. *The Study of Ethics: A Syllabus*. Ann Arbor, 1894.

For books published before 1900, you may omit the name of the publisher.

GOVERNMENT PUBLICATION

> United States. Dept. of Labor. Bur. of Statistics. *Dictionary of Occupational Titles.* 4th ed. Washington: GPO, 1977.

CHAPTER/WORK IN A ONE-AUTHOR COLLECTION

> Orwell, George. "Why I Write." *The Orwell Reader: Fiction, Essays, and Reportage by George Orwell.* New York: Harcourt, 1956. 390–96.

CHAPTER/WORK IN AN ANTHOLOGY

> Whitman, Walt. "Song of Myself." *The Norton Anthology of American Literature.* Ed. Nina Baym et al. 5th ed. vol. 1. New York: Norton, 1998. 2096–2138.

CONFERENCE PROCEEDINGS   Treat a published proceedings as a book, but add all relevant conference information.

> Harrington, Susanmarie, et al., eds. *Ninth Conference on Computers and Writing: Lessons from the Past, Learning for the Future.* Ann Arbor, May 20–23, 1993. Ann Arbor: U of Michigan P, 1993.

TWO OR MORE ITEMS IN AN ANTHOLOGY

> Baym, Nina, et al. *The Norton Anthology of American Literature.* 5th ed. 2 vols. New York: Norton, 1998.

> Whitman, Walt. "Song of Myself." Baym 1: 2096–2138.

If you are using two or more works from a collection of works by various authors, list the collection by the name of its editor and use that for cross-referencing.

ARTICLE IN A COMMON REFERENCE WORK   If the articles are alphabetically arranged, omit the volume and page numbers. Start the entry by citing the author, using the initials, usually given at the end of the article, to find the author's name from the list of contributors at the beginning of the first volume. If the article is unsigned, start the entry by citing the article title.

Don't give full publication data when citing a familiar reference book.

> Fieldhouse, David K. "Colonialism." *Encyclopedia Americana*. Int. ed. 1981.
>
> "Hayti." *Encyclopaedia Britannica*. 9th ed. 1875–89.

ARTICLE IN A SPECIALIZED REFERENCE WORK For specialized reference works (usually those that have appeared in only one or two editions), give full publication information.

> Frye, Northrop, Sheridan Baker, and George Perkins. "Classicism." *The Harper Handbook to Literature*. New York: Harper, 1985.

11d Works Cited Entries: Articles

The main divisions for each entry of an article in a periodical are as follows:

1. **Author** Give the author's last name first, then the first name, and a period.
2. **Article** State the article's full title, separating the subtitle from the title with a colon. Enclose the full title in quotation marks.
3. **Publication Information** For an article in a scholarly journal, include the *name of the journal*, in italics (underlined); the *volume number*; the *year of publication*; and the *page references*. For an article in a newspaper or magazine, include the *name of the newspaper or magazine*, in italics (underlined); the *day* (if applicable), *month* (abbreviated), and *year*; and the *page references*.

The following are variations and examples of MLA bibliographic style for citing articles in periodicals.

ARTICLE IN A SCHOLARLY/TECHNICAL PERIODICAL If each volume of a periodical is paginated continuously, give only the volume number when citing.

> Broad, William. "Rewriting the History of the H-Bomb." *Science* 218 (1982): 769–72.

If each volume of a periodical is *not* paginated continuously—that is, each issue begins with page 1—give the volume number, followed by a period and the issue number.

Posèq, Avigdor W. G. "Soutine's Two Paintings of Pigs." *Source: Notes in the History of Art* 14.2 (1995): 38–46.

If an article does not appear on successive pages—if, for example, it begins on page 21, then skips to page 23, and goes on to page 25—cite only the first page, followed by a plus sign.

Buckingham, David, and Julian Sefton-Green. "Artificial Intelligence." *Byte* Sept. 1981: 164+.

UNSIGNED ARTICLE OR COLUMN List unsigned articles or columns by title.

"Basic Principles for Managing Intellectual Property in the Digital Age." *National Humanities Alliance* 24 Mar. 1997: 1–7.

ARTICLE IN A MAGAZINE OR NEWSPAPER

Elmer-Dewitt, Philip. "On a Screen Near You: Cyberporn." *Time* 3 July 1995: 1–7.

For newspapers organized by sections, include either the section letter ("A," "B," "C," and so forth) directly before the page number ("A1+" or "D12") or the section number plus a colon directly before the page number ("sec. 1: 5+").

Eichenwald, Kurt. "Angry Chrysler Board Prevents Iacocca from Using Stock Options." *New York Times* 7 July 1995, late ed.: D1+.

REVIEW

Canby, Vincent. "The Heart of Texas." Rev. of *Places in the Heart*, dir. Robert Benton. *New York Times* 21 Sept. 1984, late ed.: C8.

Wattenberg, Martin P. "The Crisis of Electoral Politics." Rev. of *The New American Voter*, by Warren E. Miller and J. Merrill Shanks. *Atlantic Monthly* 9 July 1995: 115–120.

If the review is neither signed nor titled, begin the entry with "Rev. of," and alphabetize the entry under the title of the work being reviewed.

11e Works Cited Entries: Other Sources

PERSONAL LETTER

Bernstein, Mark. Letter to the author. 18 June 1997.

INFORMATION FROM A DOCUMENT/DATABANK

Hawes, Lorna, and Barbara Richards. *A Workshop Approach to Teaching Composition.* ERIC, 1977. ED 155 936.

Note: If the source originates from a publisher other than ERIC (Educational Resources Information Center), give the original publisher's name and date of publication before the ERIC number.

SOFTWARE

Take Note! Diskette. Palo Alto: Asymmetrix Software, 1997. (Mac or Windows 95 compatible.

After the date, you may add other relevant information, such as operating-system requirements.

TV/RADIO PROGRAM

"Rubinstein Remembered: A One-Hundredth Anniversary Tribute." *American Masters.* Narr. John Rubinstein. PBS. WBIQ, Birmingham, AL. 17 July 1987.

After the title of episode (if known) and program, give the names of those chiefly responsible for it.

RECORDING   Alphabetize recordings under whatever element you wish to emphasize the most, ending with the manufacturer and the year of issue.

Aïda. By Giuseppe Verdi. With Birgit Nilsson, Franco Corelli, Grace Bumbry, and Mario Sereni. Cond. Zubin Mehta.

Orchestra and Chorus of the Opera House, Rome. LPs. Angel,
n.d.

Bartoli, Cecilia. "Voi che sapete." By Wolfgang Amadeus Mozart.
Mozart Arias. London, 1991.

FILM Alphabetize either by film title or by principal individual.

Schindler's List. Dir. Steven Spielberg. Perf. Liam Neeson, Ben
Kingsley, and Ralph Fiennes. Universal, 1993.

Spielberg, Steven, dir. *Schindler's List.* Perf. Liam Neeson, Ben
Kingsley, and Ralph Fiennes. Universal, 1993.

PERFORMANCE

Misalliance. By George Bernard Shaw. Dir. Tony Van Bridge. Perf.
Nancy Boykin, Betty Leighton, and Kermit Brown. Alabama
Shakespeare Festival, Montgomery. 4 July 1987.

INTERVIEW To cite an interview that you conducted, include
in the entry the name of the interviewee, the type of interview
(personal, telephone), and the date.

Peterson, Jon. Telephone interview. 23 July 1998.

If the interview has been published or broadcast, give the relevant bibliographic information in the appropriate form.

Kundera, Milan. Interview. *New York Times* 18 Jan. 1982, sec. 3:
13+.

ELECTRONIC SOURCES Works Cited entries for electronic
sources should include the basic information that is standard
for print sources. Specific guidelines are given below for different kinds of electronic sources. MLA's recommendations for
electronic citation, which we follow, are available on the Web
at ⟨www.mla.org⟩. For updates to this chapter, check the Writing Essentials Website ⟨http://www.wwnorton.com/WE⟩. Since
online citation issues are still in flux, you may also want to
check with your teacher before adopting these guidelines.

1. **Author** Give the author's name, last name first.
2. **Title** For articles, give the full title of the article or doc-

ument in quotation marks. For full texts, italicize (underline) the title.

3. **Publication Information**   This varies, depending on the electronic source. See the guidelines, below. *Note:* (1) Use angle brackets, ⟨ ⟩, around URLs (Web addresses) because they make the URL easy to spot and because they allow use of a period at the end of the citation—for example ⟨http://www.wwnorton.com/WE⟩. Without the angle brackets, many users are not sure whether the period at the end of the sentence is part of the URL. If the URL spans more than one line, divide it at a slash (/) mark. (2) If there is no date available, omit the date or type "n.d." for "no date."

World Wide Web

References to Websites available to the general public should include the author, title of publication and/or Web page, date of publication, your access date, and the Web address (URL) in angle brackets.

> Noguera, Pedro. "A Popular Movement for Social Justice." *In Motion Magazine* 1996. 21 July 1997. ⟨http://www.inmotionmagazine.com/pedro2.html⟩.

> Wayner, Peter. "Internet Glitch Reveals System's Pervasiveness, Vulnerability." *New York Times Online*. Online. 10 July 1997. 18 July 1997 ⟨http://www.nytimes.com⟩.

Internet Listserv

References to an Internet Listserv should include the author, the title from the subject line of the message, date of posting, your access date, and either the Listserv subscription information or the Web address (URL), in angle brackets, of the Listserv archive, if available.

> Rodrigues, Dawn. "Eastgate Software." 28 May 1997. 6 June 1998. ACW-l. Internet Listserv. ⟨http://ttuvm1.ttu.edu/acw-l.htm⟩.

Personal E-mail correspondence

> Madden, Frank. "Ocean Creek Conference." E-mail to author. 14 June 1997.

Online databases

References to proprietary online databases (such as Lexis/Nexis, ABI/INFORM, or InfoSeek) or to databases available through online services (such as America Online or CompuServe), or

CD-ROM databases should include the author, title, name of the serial or database (journal, newspaper, and so forth), publication information (date, volume and number, page numbers), access date (for Web sources but not CD-ROM), electronic publishing information (online service, name of database, publisher of CD-ROM source, Web URL for Web sources), and access or record number if available.

Casse, Daniel. "Why Welfare Reform Is Working." *Commentary* 104.3 (1997): 36–42. OVID. 12 Feb. 1998 〈http://www.ovid.com〉. Access Number: 0003392862.

Perelman, Les. "School's Out." *Wired Magazine* 3 Jan. 1993. America Online. 28 July 1998.

Other electronic publications
References to other electronic publications (such as computer programs) should be treated as if they were books: give the author (if available), the title, the publishing company, and the date of publication. After the title, indicate the type of electronic publication (diskette, CD-ROM, videodisc, and so forth).

Perseus 1.0: Interactive Sources and Studies on Ancient Greece. CD-ROM, videodisc. New Haven: Yale UP, 1992.

Tracking Online Sources ONLINE TIP

- Use bookmarks or bookmark files to organize valuable online sources. Save your bookmarks to a floppy disk; open the bookmark file as a Web page (select "open local page" with your browser, and then open the file named "Bookmark" or whatever you renamed the bookmark file).
- Create note cards that summarize online sources. Include the date of access and the specific medium (America Online, the Internet, or a CD-ROM) used to locate the source. In the case of CD-ROMs, include the publishing company and the publication date. *Note:* If you print the Web pages you plan to cite, the URL will usually be included in the upper right-hand corner of each printed page.
- Set up a table to track Internet sources you plan to use:
  Author: Price, Rick
  Title: Censorship on the Web
  Volume number and issue and page numbers, if any:
  Publisher or URL and date of publication: 〈http://linux2.mur.csu.edu/au/≈rprice01/index.htm〉
  Access date: May 26, 1997

12 APA Documentation

APA style, often used in the social sciences, consists of in-text citations that refer readers to a list of references at the end of a paper.

12a In-Text Citation Format

APA citation requires three pieces of information, which are placed either in the text or in parentheses:

1. The source of the article, usually the name(s) of the author(s)
2. The date of publication
3. The page number(s) in that source

If you are citing the entire source, you can omit the page numbers.

ONE WORK BY ONE AUTHOR   Include the author's last name either in the text or within parentheses, separated by a comma from the year of publication. Add a page reference if you are referring to a specific part of a reference. Here are two rules to keep in mind:

1. When including a page reference, make sure that the date is followed by a comma and that the abbreviation "p." or "pp." precedes the page number.
2. When you refer to the author, either in the text or in parentheses, use the *last name only*.

   ▶ Although computers may lead to many improvements in education, critics contend that computers lack the ability to provide a "cure for ills that are social and political in nature" (Roszak, 1986).

   ▶ Roszak (1986) discusses the limitations of computers to cure social ills.

The above format is often used when you do not want to cite specific pages.

   ▶ Although computers may lead to many improvements in education, one computer critic contends that they lack the ability to provide a "cure for ills that are social and political in nature" (Roszak, 1986, p. 216).

APA Quick Reference

TWO OR MORE WORKS BY ONE AUTHOR If you have two or more works by the same author, the year of publication is often enough to differentiate one work from another. If two or more works were written in the same year, distinguish among them by adding "a," "b," "c," and so forth after the year.

▶ Bruner, 1986a
  Bruner, 1986b

If the above works were included in the same paper, "Bruner, 1986a" would refer to "Bruner, J. (1986). *Actual minds, possible worlds*"; "Bruner, 1986b" would refer to "Bruner, J. (1986). *A study of thinking.*"

ONE WORK WITH TWO OR MORE AUTHORS With two authors, include the last names of *both* for all citations, using an ampersand (&) instead of the word *and* between the names. Follow the names with a comma and the date of publication.

> ▶ All writing has the potential of being creative (Bishop & Ostrom, 1994).

With three to five authors, give the name of each author for the first reference and, for subsequent citations, the name of the first author only, followed by "et al." ("and others") and the year.

FIRST CITATION

> ▶ Brooke, Levin, and Stanley (1994) argue . . .

> ▶ . . . (Brooke, Levin, & Stanley, 1994).

SUBSEQUENT CITATIONS

> ▶ Brooke et al. (1994) argue . . .

> ▶ . . . as has been argued (Brooke et al., 1994).

With six or more authors, use the last name of only the *first* author followed by "et al." for all textual references, but list *all* the authors in the reference list.

> ▶ But Jones et al. (1994) maintain . . .

CORPORATE AUTHOR The names of corporate authors are usually spelled out each time they appear in the text. However, corporate authors with long names or with familiar abbreviations may be shortened after the first citation.

FIRST CITATION

> ▶ . . . AIDS research (National Institutes of Health [NIH], 1998).

Note: Brackets are used to enclose the abbreviation because the item itself is enclosed in parentheses.

SUBSEQUENT CITATIONS

> ▶ . . . future plans (NIH, 1998).

NO AUTHOR OR ANONYMOUS If a work has no author, cite in the text the first two or three words of the title, using quotation marks or italics (underlining) for articles and books, respectively; then give the year.

▶ Another source (*College Cost Book*, 1998) notes . . .

▶ As the *College Cost Book* (1998) notes, . . .

AUTHOR QUOTED BY ANOTHER SOURCE

▶ Lovely notes that overly narrow and regimented computerized research in astronomy is damaging to "the free exercise of that happy faculty known as serendipity" (as quoted in Roszak, 1989, p. 115).

AUTHORS WITH THE SAME NAME   If your reference list includes two or more authors with the same last name, include the authors' initials in all textual references, even if the years of publication differ.

▶ As R. A. Adams (1986) and P. B. Adams (1989) both contend, . . .

TWO OR MORE WORKS IN ONE CITATION   List the parenthetical citations to two or more sources alphabetically, just as in they appear in the reference list. List two or more works by a single author chronologically.

▶ . . . appears promising (Bishop & Ostrom, 1994; Brooke, Levin, & Stanley, 1994).

▶ Past research (Britton, 1972, 1985) . . .

PART OF A SOURCE   Include a page number or other appropriate reference when referring to a specific part of a work. Acceptable APA abbreviations for parts of a publication include "chap." ("chapter"), "No." ("Number"), "p." and "pp." ("page" and "pages"), and "Vol." ("Volume," as in "Vol. 2").

▶ Although computers may lead to many improvements in education, critics contend that they lack the ability to provide a "cure for ills that are social and political in nature" (Roszak, 1986, p. 219).

PERSONAL COMMUNICATION   Cite personal communication only in the text, not in the References.

▶ The Literature and Technology Institute was well received by participants (P. Stock, personal communication, June 7, 1997).

ELECTRONIC SOURCES References to electronic sources are handled much as references to books and journals: if you indicate the author or title in your sentence, you do not need to include it in the parenthetical citation. If you do not mention the author, title, or date, then you do need to include appropriate information in parentheses at the end of the sentence. Provide as much context for your source as possible in your sentence: For Internet sources, provide the address of the Web page (the URL). For CD-ROMs, indicate the publisher and publication date. For subscription databases, indicate the Web address or the CD-ROM information. Keep in mind that APA treats E-mail as personal communication. Thus, E-mail sources are not listed in the References (unless your teacher specifically asks you to do so).

▶ In *Censorship on the Web* (1997), Rick Price provides an excellent collection of resources on the topic of Web censorship.

▶ The Online Writing Center at Colorado State University provides tutorials for writing research papers (Palmquist, 1997).

▶ Students enjoyed using E-mail in my English course. Sandra Smith explained that "it feels more like talking to classmates" (personal E-mail communication, June 15, 1995).

12b References

Starting on a new page entitled References and using the APA style, list all the works you have cited. APA recommends a "hanging indent" format for final typeset copy but suggests standard paragraph indentions for student papers. This suggestion has come about because of the difficulty people have had creating hanging indents with their word processing programs. If hanging indents are relatively easy to create in your word processing program (and if your teacher allows), you can use hanging indents in your final draft. For more information, see ⟨http://www.apa.org⟩.

Arrange entries alphabetically by the author's last name or, when you have no author's name, by the first significant word in the title. When you have several works by the same author, list the entries chronologically, starting with the earliest publication. When you have several works by the same author with the same publication date, arrange the entries alphabetically by title and use the lowercase letters "a," "b," "c," and so forth after the year and within the parentheses.

12c References Entries: Books

The main divisions for each book entry are as follows:

1. **Author** Give the author's last name first, followed by a comma, then the initials.
2. **Date** Put the date of publication within parentheses.
3. **Title** Italicize (underline) the full title. Capitalize only the first word of the title and subtitle as well as all proper nouns.
4. **Publication Information** Include the *place of publication*, then the *publisher*.
   - When citing a publisher's location, give the city and, if the city is not well known, state for U.S. publishers and the city and, if needed, country for foreign publishers. If more than one city of publication is listed in a book, give the first one only.
   - You may shorten the name of a well-known publisher ("Norton" instead of "W. W. Norton & Company").

The following are variations and/or examples of APA bibliographic style for citing books.

BOOK WITH ONE AUTHOR OR EDITOR Capitalize the first word of the title and subtitle, and any proper names; italicize (underline) the entire title.

Erikson, E. H. (Ed.). (1978). *Adulthood*. New York: Norton.

Lesser, G. S. (1974). *Children and television: Lessons from Sesame Street*. New York: Random House.

BOOK WITH TWO OR MORE AUTHORS OR EDITORS Give in inverted form the names of *all* the authors in the order listed on the title page, inserting an ampersand (&) just before the last author.

Gemmill, E., & Mayhew, N. (1995). *Changing values in medieval Scotland: A study of prices, money, and weights and measures*. Cambridge: Cambridge University Press.

REVISED EDITION OF A BOOK Abbreviate the edition ("2nd," "Rev.," "Enl.") as indicated on its title page.

O'Connor, F. (1995). Guests of the Nation. In R. V. Cassill (Ed.), *The Norton anthology of short fiction* (5th ed., pp. 1227–1235). New York: Norton.

BOOK WITH A CORPORATE AUTHOR Alphabetize corporate authors by the first significant word of the name. When the author and publisher are the same, use "Author" where the publisher's name would appear.

American Psychological Association. (1995). *Publication manual of the American Psychological Association* (4th ed.). Washington, DC: Author.

BOOK WITH NO AUTHOR Alphabetize under the first significant word in the title. Thus, in the following example, the entry would be alphabetized under "Nineteen."

The 1995 NEA almanac of higher education. (1995). Washington, DC: National Education Association.

BOOK WITH TWO OR MORE VOLUMES

Eisenstein, E. L. (1979). *The printing press as an agent of change* (Vols. 1–2). New York: Cambridge University Press.

BOOK IN TRANSLATION

Kristeva, J. (1987). *In the beginning was love: Psychonalysis and faith.* (Arthur Goldhammer, Trans.). New York: Columbia University Press.

GOVERNMENT DOCUMENT

National Institute of Mental Health. (1982). *Television and behavior: Ten years of scientific progress and implications for the eighties* (DHHS Publication No. ADM 82-1195). Washington, DC: U.S. Government Printing Office.

ARTICLE IN A ONE-AUTHOR COLLECTION

Orwell, G. (1956). Why I write. In *The Orwell reader: Fiction, essays, and reportage by George Orwell* (pp. 390–396). New York: Harcourt.

ARTICLE/CHAPTER IN AN EDITED COLLECTION

Walhstrom, B. (1994). Communication and technology: Defining a feminist presence in research and practice. In C. Selfe & S.

Hilligoss (Eds.), *Literacy and computers: The complications of teaching and learning with technology* (pp. 171–185). New York: MLA.

ARTICLE/CHAPTER IN A REFERENCE WORK

Frye, N., Baker, S., & Perkins, G. (1985). Classicism. In *The Harper handbook to literature* (p. 105). New York: Harper.

12d References Entries: Articles

The main divisions for each entry of an article in a periodical are as follows:

1. **Author** Give the author's last name first, then the initials. If there is more than one author, list them all, and insert an ampersand (&) before the last author.
2. **Date of Publication** Place the year of publication within parentheses. If you are citing a daily, weekly, or monthly periodical, include the month and, if applicable, the day within the parentheses after the year.
3. **Article** State the article's full title, capitalizing only the first word of the title and subtitle as well as all proper nouns. Do not italicize (underline) the full title or use quotation marks around it.
4. **Publication Information** This part of the entry should include the *name of the periodical* in italics (underlined), the *volume number* in italics (underlined), and the *page references*, using "pp." only before newspaper citations.

The following are variations and/or examples of APA bibliographic style for citing articles in periodicals.

ARTICLE IN AN ACADEMIC JOURNAL

Harris, M. (1989). Composing behaviors of one- and multi-draft writers. *College English, 51,* 174–191.

If each issue is paginated separately, include the issue number in parentheses immediately after the volume number, leaving no space between the two elements. Do not italicize (underline) the issue number.

Journal of Social Issues, 37(2), 1–7.

ARTICLE/CHAPTER IN AN ANNUAL   Treat annuals with regular publication dates as periodicals, not books.

> Kessler, R. C., Price, R. H., & Wortman, C. B. (1985). Social factors in psychotherapy: Stress, social support, and coping processes. *Annual Review of Psychology, 36*, 531–572.

MAGAZINE ARTICLE

> Kreilkamp, Ivan (1998, June 29). Pagan Kennedy: From 'zine to mainstream. *Publishers Weekly, 245*, 31–32.

NEWSPAPER EDITORIAL

> China: Kind words, little effect. (1995, August 7). [Editorial]. *The New York Times*, p. A12.

12e References Entries: Other Sources

MATERIAL FROM AN INFORMATION SERVICE

> Couture, B. (1993). Against relativism: Restoring truth in writing. *Journal of Advanced Composition, 13*(1), 111–134. (ERIC Document Reproduction Service No. EJ 455 641)

FILM

> Benton, R. (Director). (1984). *Places in the heart* [Film]. Los Angeles: Tri-Star.

ELECTRONIC SOURCES   The American Psychological Association (APA) has begun to develop guidelines for electronic citation, but the guidelines only account for a few of the many kinds of sources used by students. We have, therefore, chosen to follow and adapt the more comprehensive model for APA presented by Xia Li and Nancy B. Crane in *Electronic Styles: A Handbook for Citing Electronic Information*, 2nd ed. (Medford, NJ: Information Today, 1997). For updates to this chapter, check the *Writing Essentials* Website ⟨http://www.wwnorton.com/ WE⟩.

Full citations in the References section contain the author, the date of publication, the title of the source, and the name of the periodical or work with volume and page numbers, if applicable. This information is followed by type of electronic source, database, or service (America Online, ERIC, CD-ROM). If the information is available on the Internet or from a computer service, type "Available:" followed by the Internet address (the URL) or the name of the computer service. Note that personal communication such as E-mail is not included in the References; in-text citation is sufficient.

World Wide Web

Borjas, G. (1996, November). The new economics of immigration. *The Atlantic Monthly* [Online], *278*(5), 72–80. Available: http://www2.theAtlantic.com [1997, July 23].

Pritzker, T. J. (No date). *An early fragment from central Nepal.* [Online]. Available http://www.ingress.com/~astanart/pritzker/pritzker.html [1995, June 8].

Internet Listserv

DRODRIGUES (1997, June 6). Eastgate software. Alliance for Computers and Writing Listserv. [Online]. Available: http://english.ttu.edu/acw/acw-l/archive.htm [1997, June 6].

Note: Providing the author's login name allows someone wanting to retrieve the source to search a Listserv archive for the username.

CD-ROM or Internet-accessible database

Oates, J. C. (1998, Winter). The action of mercy. *The Kenyon Review* [Online], *20*(1), 157–60. Available: http://www.proquest.umi.com [1998, May 10]. Access number: 03526155.

Oxford English Dictionary computer file: On compact disc (2nd ed.), [CD-ROM]. (1992). Available: Oxford UP [1995, May 27].

Sleek, S. (1996, January). Psychologists build a culture of peace. *APA Monitor* [CD-ROM], 1, 33. Available: http://www.apa.org/monitor/peacea.html [1996, January 25].

Note: When these guidelines were written, most databases were only available on CD-ROM. This model follows our recommendation for citing an online database; check with your teacher for alternate instructions.

E-Mail

APA does not require that you cite E-mail in your References. Check with your instructor.

13 CBE Documentation

The Council of Biology Editors manual, *Scientific Style and Format*, describes two methods of documentation: the name-year system and the citation-sequence system. These systems are often used by writers in the natural sciences. For more information about CBE style, see the *Writing Essentials* Website, ⟨http://www.wwnorton.com/WE⟩.

13a Name-Year System

The name-year system refers to the practice of including the author(s) and the date of publication in parentheses in the text. This system is similar to the APA style except that it uses *and* between authors names instead of the ampersand (&) and does not use a comma between author(s) and the date of publication.

► These researchers (Westone and Rosencrantz 1983) have analyzed acid rain in many countries across the world.

► White-lined bark beetles are attracted to the odor of rotting wood (Zorn and others 1992).

► Wylie (1978, 1979, 1983) describes the circulatory system in detail.

13b Citation-Sequence System

In the citation-sequence system, each reference is numbered (in superscript) at the point in the sentence where the source is mentioned. Subsequent references to the same source should be given the same number. Thus, if you have several references to the same book, each reference in the text has the same number.

► Westone[1] and Rosencrantz[2] have analyzed acid rain in many countries across the world.

► White-lined bark beetles are attracted to the odor of rotting wood,[3] which is more prominent in areas with considerable acid rain.[1,2]

▶ Wylie[4,1,6] describes the circulatory system in detail.

13c References or Cited References

In the name-year system, list your references in alphabetical order at the end of your text. In the citation-sequence system, first number the items in your reference list in the order in which they appear in the text, and then arrange them in that order. Abbreviate page ranges: for example, if you want to cite an article that spans pages 42 to 46, indicate the page range by writing "42–6." For electronic sources, indicate specific types of source in brackets: "[serial online]," "[monograph online]," "[book online]," and so forth.

The following are examples of reference entries using the citation-sequence system.

BOOK

1 Schmandt J. Acid rain and friendly neighbors: the policy dispute between Canada and the United States. Durham: Duke Univ. Pr; 1989. p. 166.

JOURNAL ARTICLE

2 Brush SG. Women in science and engineering. Am Sci 1991; 79(5):404–19.

ELECTRONIC SOURCES

3 Shaohua Z. A tool for visualizing and manipulating geophysical data [serial online] 1996 May 29. Available from: http://www. the-scientist.library.upenn.edu/yr1996/feb/malthus_960205.html. Accessed 1998 Mar 3.

4 Kupisch SJ. Stepping in. Paper presented at the annual meeting of the Southeastern Psychological Association, Atlanta, GA, 1983 Mar 23–6. Dialog, ERIC, ED 233276.

ABSTRACT

5 Bowen WG, Rudenstine NL. In pursuit of the Ph.D [abstract]. In: Princeton University Press Catalog; 1992. Available from: http:// pup.princeton.edu/titles/4957.html. Accessed 1998 Mar 3.

6 Mendez MF, Manon-Espaillat R, Lanska DJ, Burstine TH. Epilepsy and suicide attempts [abstract]. In: American Academy of Neurology 41st annual meeting program; 1989 Apr 13–19; Chicago. Cleveland (OH): Edgell Communications; 1989. p 295. Abstract nr PP369.

GOVERNMENT DOCUMENT

7 National Wildlife Federation (US). Acid rain: its state by state impacts. Washington: National Technical Information Service; 1984.

14 Turabian Documentation

Kate L. Turabian, in the sixth edition of her *Manual for Writers of Term Papers, Theses, and Dissertations* (1996), offers stylistic advice for the note system of documentation as well as for parenthetical citation.

14a Note System

Key features of the note system include the following:

- Consecutively number your notes throughout your text. Use a superscript (raised number) to indicate where each note belongs in your text.

  ▶ Rodrigues and Tuman[1] provide additional information about citation styles at their Website. Other Norton publications, such as *Web Works*,[2] also have Websites.

- In footnotes or endnotes, list citations in the order cited, but use numbers followed by a period rather than superscript numbers. Place footnotes at the bottom of each page (directly under a 1- to 2-inch horizontal line situated at the left-hand margin) unless your instructor allows endnotes (a list of notes on a separate page at the end of your paper).

  ▶ 1. Dawn Rodrigues and Myron Tuman, *Writing Essentials*, 2d ed. (New York: Norton, 1999), 67.

  ▶ 2. Martin Irvine, *Web Works* (New York: Norton, 1997).

- For second and subsequent references, use a shortened form of the full note: either "ibid." or "Rodrigues and Tuman, 32."
- Abbreviate page ranges: for example, if you want to cite an article that spans pages 42 to 46, indicate the page range by writing "42–46."

14b Parenthetical System

Key features of the parenthetical citation style include the following:

- List the author's last name and date unless any of these items are mentioned in the text itself.

  ▶ . . . (Rodrigues and Tuman 1999).

- Quotations from specific pages should be cited by page number.

  ▶ . . . (Rodrigues and Tuman 1999, 73).

- When titles and names of documents are used as the "author," they are capitalized in the same way as they were originally published.
- If the author has published several books or other publications, differentiate by date only.

  ▶ . . . Smith's studies (1995, 1996).

- If, however, two or more works by the same author have the same publication date, add "a," "b," "c," and so forth to these dates.

  ▶ . . . (Keller 1896a, 1896b, 1907).

14c Works Cited or References

List the sources you have used in your paper in alphabetical order on a separate page called either Works Cited (note system) or References (parenthetical system). List only the works that you have cited, not those that you have used for background information. Should you wish to include background sources, call your list Selected Bibliography.

Using the examples that follow, compare the styles of the two bibliographic systems.

BOOK

Forster, B. A. 1993. *The acid rain debate: Science and special interests in policy formation.* Ames: Iowa State University Press.   [*parenthetical system*]

Forster, Bruce A. *The Acid Rain Debate: Science and Special Interests in Policy Formation.* Ames: Iowa State University Press, 1993.   [*note system*]

JOURNAL ARTICLE

Rosenblatt, Louise M. 1993. The transactional theory: Against dualisms. *College English* 55:377–86.   [*parenthetical system*]

Rosenblatt, Louise M. "The Transactional Theory: Against Dualisms." *College English* 55 (1993): 377–86.   [*note system*]

GOVERNMENT DOCUMENT

National Wildlife Federation. 1984. *Acid rain: Its state by state impacts.* Washington, D.C.: U.S. Department of Commerce.   [*parenthetical system*]

National Wildlife Federation. *Acid Rain: Its State by State Impacts.* Washington, D.C.: U.S. Department of Commerce, 1984.   [*note system*]

ELECTRONIC SOURCES

Shaohua, Zhou. 1998. *A tool for visualizing and manipulating geophysical data.* American Geophysical Union. Serial online. Accessed 1998 March 15. Available from ⟨http://www.agu.org/eos_elec⟩.   [*parenthetical system*]

Shaohua, Zhou. *A Tool for Visualizing and Manipulating Geophysical Data.* American Geophysical Union, 1998. Serial online. Accessed 1998 March 15. Available from ⟨http://www.agu.org/eos_elec⟩.   [*note system*]

Kupisch, Susan J. 1983. *Stepping in.* Paper presented at the annual meeting of the Southeastern Psychological Association, Atlanta, Ga., 23–26 March. Dialog, ERIC, ED 233 276.   [*parenthetical system*]

Kupisch, Susan J. *Stepping In.* Paper presented at the annual meeting of the Southeastern Psychological Association, Atlanta, Ga., 23–26 March 1983. Dialog, ERIC ED 233 276.   [*note system*]

Basic
Document
Design

15 Document and Page Design

For years, guides like this one offered only the briefest advice about the appearance of college papers. Most notable were instructions to students to use standard 8 × 11-inch paper, to leave 1-inch margins on all four sides, to double-space between lines, and to clean their typewriter keys before typing their paper. The assumption was that, if this writing were ever to be published, someone else (not the writer, but a designer or compositor) would be responsible for how that writing looked on the printed page. Meanwhile, the few things that student writers had to do—like putting their name and page number at the top right of each page, starting with page 2, or setting a new, temporary left margin—they did manually.

All this changed with word processing and is about to change even more with the growing popularity of the World Wide Web. Writers now have the ability to control not only the words on the page, but also the appearance of those words. While the goal of producing a neat, legible text remains, even the most basic commands for preparing printed copy are now entered as software instructions, as is the case with the title and page number that appear in a running header. Meanwhile, nearly all word processing programs give you the tools to control many other aspects of how your printed paper will look, especially when used in conjunction with a laser printer. While few teachers may expect you to master all the features necessary to produce professional-looking printed documents or Web pages, you should understand the fundamentals of document design that determine the appearance of both printed or Web texts.

15a Printed Documents

WORD PROCESSING DEFAULT SETTINGS Although laser printers and sophisticated word processors give you considerable control over the appearance of your documents, in most cases you can produce acceptable documents using the default settings on your word processor. Programs generally assume

- standard 8 × 11-inch paper in portrait (long), as compared to landscape (wide), page orientation
- no multiple columns
- printing on one side of the paper only
- a minimum 1-inch margin on all four sides

Even with these default settings, you will still need to control formatting options in three areas:

- headers and page numbering
- paragraph margins
- fonts and typefaces

HEADINGS AND HEADERS, TITLE PAGES, AND PAGE NUMBER-ING With all college essays, you are required to supply certain information once, at the beginning of the paper itself, usually starting on the first line of text of the first page and flush with the left margin. This information, called a heading, ordinarily consists of

- your name
- your teacher's name
- the course name and number
- the due date of the assignment

On *all* the pages of your paper, you need to include a header (so called because it appears at the top of each page, above the first line of text), which contains your last name and the current page. See the paper on pages 51–54 for style.

Normally, you would enter the heading that appears on page 1 of your paper as regular text. For headers that appear automatically on subsequent pages and include your name and the page number, you must use a special word processing command.

Separate title pages are not normally required for college papers. Check with your instructor for guidelines, if you are required to prepare one. As a general rule, a title page will contain the title at the top, center of the page, followed by the same information as in a heading: your name, your teacher's name, the course name and number, the due date of the assignment—all centered. You would then normally repeat your title on the first page of your text, centered at the top, and start your header, with last name and current page number, on the next page (page 2).

OTHER PAGE-NUMBERING OPTIONS Certain disciplines may require the use of additional numbering systems in formal research papers—for example, the use of lower-case Roman numerals for introductory material or Arabic numerals placed as footers (information that appears at the bottom of every page) on the first page of every new chapter.

PARAGRAPH MARGINS There are two important things to note about word processing paragraphs. First, a paragraph in word processing is purely a technical entity that consists of all text between end-of-paragraph markers—the space or character you create each time you press ENTER in most word processing programs. Thus, a Works Cited entry is technically one paragraph—as is your name, the date, and other information at the top of page 1—simply because you have pressed ENTER to move to the next line.

Second, most paragraphs have two different left margins: one setting for the first line (the line immediately below the last end-of-paragraph marker) and another setting for all subsequent lines of text. The first line of text is sometimes called the paragraph margin, as compared to the normal left margin for all subsequent lines of text.

LEFT MARGINS AND EXTENDED QUOTATIONS All word processing programs allow you to reset the left margins temporarily, another function you should master. There are at least two places where you will need to change the left paragraph margins in a college essay: in extended quotations, where the left margin is moved in 1 inch, and in the Works Cited section of your paper (if you are following MLA style), which uses a hanging margin or hanging indent, in which the first line of each citation is flush left and all subsequent lines are indented. You also need a 1-inch indented left margin whenever you are quoting three or more lines of poetry. Remember to retain the poem's own indentions and different margin settings.

The relationship between the paragraph margin and the regular left margin results in the following different types, or shapes, of paragraphs:

Indented paragraph

The confrontation with Miss Ivors is not the only one that causes a change in Gabriel Conroy. After the party, he and Gretta retire to their hotel room. Gabriel is filled with desire for his wife, but he is disappointed when they arrive at the room. Gretta has no thoughts of making love to her husband. . . .

In "The Daughters of the Late Colonel," Katherine Mansfield presents a story of two girls who are faced with great change after the death of their father. . . .

Block paragraph

Please consider my application for the part-time intern position in your new community outreach program. I am both trained and ready to do such work.

As part of a social-work course I am taking this term, I have served seventy-five hours as a volunteer at the Reich Senior Citizens Center. . . .

Hanging paragraph

Bolter, J. David. *Turing's Man: Western Culture in the Computer Age.* Chapel Hill: U of North Carolina P, 1984.
Brand, Stewart. *The Media Lab: Inventing the Future at MIT.* New York: Viking, 1987.

RIGHT MARGINS The design of most professional publications usually includes aligned, or justified right margins. For college essays, however, most readers prefer the normal fixed spacing between words that results in an unjustified, or ragged, right margin

LINE SPACING AND PARAGRAPH MARGINS Indented paragraphs work well with double-spaced text, the traditional form for college essays that were intended to be notated by instructors in print form. This extra line space created by double spacing is not necessary, however, when the instructor is responding to and annotating papers online. If you submit your papers electronically, your instructor may prefer that you use block paragraphs with the text single-spaced and a blank line added between paragraphs.

OTHER FORMATTING FEATURES Word processing programs today permit users to integrate illustrations directly into their text, often allowing the text to wrap around the picture. Whether you take advantage of this feature or not, be sure to number all illustrations sequentially (Illustration 1, Illustration 2, and so forth). Also, supply a brief caption for each illustration as well as a brief in-text reference to each, by number.

The use of varied fonts and graphics along with the ability to lay out and print text in multiple columns allows users to produce a wide range of attractive, professional-looking newsletters and other nontraditional academic documents. Students producing such documents in the future will need different, more extensive guidelines about document design than students writing traditional research papers.

FORCED PAGE BREAK All word processing programs have a command to end the current page and start a new one (sometimes called a hard page break)—for example, at the end of a separate title page. Some programs also have a special command, called a conditional page break, that only breaks a page when there is a limited amount of space left at the start of a new paragraph. Either form of page break allows you to keep important information together on a single page.

HARD SPACES Word processing programs may break lines between phrases, terms, or names such as "Los Angeles" or "Dr. Jones," or between the periods that form an ellipsis. To prevent this from happening, you must insert a hard space instead of simply using the spacebar.

HYPHENS—REGULAR, SOFT, HARD Word processing calls for three kinds of hyphens, all of which look the same when printed but must be entered differently in the editing stage.

- **Regular hyphen:** used to allow the program to decide when to break a hyphenated word (like *self-important*) at the end of a line
- **Soft hyphen:** used to break a word at the end of a line (called *soft* since it disappears if the format of the document changes and the word is no longer divided between two lines)
- **Hard hyphen:** used to keep a two-part, hyphenated term (like the phone number 500-1286) from breaking at the end of a line (so called since it bonds itself to the next character)

DASH   With typewriters, people form a dash by using two hyphens; using two hyphens with a word processor can create a small problem, however, if during automatic formatting of text the program allows the line to break between the two hyphens. There are two ways to avoid this:

- Use a hard hyphen followed by a regular hyphen to create the dash.
- Use the function of most word processing programs that allows you to insert special characters, here a **true dash**, **solid dash**, or **em dash** (—), instead of two hyphens (--).

TABS   To shift a fixed distance left or right or to move any line, you must use the tab settings of your word processing program, not the spacebar. This is especially true if you are using a proportional font, in which case the spacebar has no fixed value. Becoming comfortable with setting and moving tabs takes time and practice. So find this feature on your word processing program, and begin to use it.

Designing a Resume ▸ ONLINE TIP

The two parts of a resume are fairly simple and straightforward: centered individual lines that include name, address, and telephone number; individual lines that feature a category (like "Education") at the left margin, followed by two tab stops—for example, one at 2.5 inches and the other at 3.5 inches—the first for the years and the second for a description or explanation. *Note:* You may have to adjust your tab settings to get the right spacing. Below is a sample.

Linda Forbes
1219 West Eagle Street
Linden, AL 35678
205-752-0871

Education	1997	University of Alabama, B.A.
Experience	1996	Organized and charted records for University Health Service. Served as a community volunteer for local United Way agency.

When the explanatory text runs over to two or more lines, switch to a hanging-paragraph format for the body of the resume, perhaps with the paragraph margin at 1 inch and the left margin at 3 inches. Then set the first tab stop to 3 inches as well.

15b Fonts, Typefaces, and Headings

Before computers, writers often made just one decision about typefaces: whether to get a typewriter with pica type (large— 10 characters per inch) or elite type (small—12 characters per inch). Today, with computer-generated type at your disposal, laser printers for reproducing hard copy, and the World Wide Web for displaying online texts, all of us have many more options when it comes to printing or otherwise displaying documents, although it may well be the case that the teachers evaluating your work and even others who may be reading it still care about documents being clear and legible. Unless your teacher advises otherwises, therefore, the best advice is not to take time away from revising your paper in order to improve its appearance. What follows are some of the basics you need to understand about fonts and typefaces.

PROPORTIONAL AND FIXED FONTS   Typewriters and many old-fashioned computer programs work with fixed fonts, whereas most new computer programs regularly display and print the kind of proportional fonts long associated with professional publications. With proportional fonts, the width of individual letters appearing on the screen or paper varies, the eight letters of *Illinois* (proportional) occupying considerably less space than the seven letters of Wyoming (fixed). Hence, changing your paper from a fixed to a proportional font will decrease its length by as much as a third, and vice versa, meaning that word count, not page numbers, is now the only reliable way to measure paper length.

FONT SIZE AND STYLE   Fonts are measured in points, with 72 points to an inch. College documents are traditionally prepared using 12-point fonts (the size of pica type), while the smaller 10-point fonts (the size of elite type) are usually preferred for personal correspondence or where it may be important to fit more text on a single page. For most academic writing, use large or boldface fonts sparingly, and then mainly for titles or for subtitles within papers (as in the multiple headings used in scientific documents), since they can overwhelm a document.

The small cross strokes at the ends of the main strokes of individual letters (for example, M) are called serifs, and the most popular of the serif fonts (associated with newspapers and books generally) is Times Roman. Sans serif, the style of type without cross strokes (for example, **M**), such as Univers, have a less traditional or formal look. While either is appropriate for academic writing, be careful in varying your font within a paper, introducing a new one only when truly needed.

LINE SPACING   The space between lines within a paragraph is set automatically by word processing programs and is based on the size of the default font. Most people use the ENTER key to insert extra lines manually between block paragraphs. You may also be able to change the amount of space the program leaves before and after each paragraph by editing the style or description of the paragraph type.

PARAGRAPH STYLES   Most word processing programs allow you to predefine paragraph types according to their shape (the three margins discussed on page 93), their default font type and size, tab stops, and the line spacing within as well as before and after the paragraph. Headings, discussed below, can be thought of as single-line paragraph styles, usually using display type with extra space before and after each paragraph.

HEADINGS   While academic papers are always composed of subsections, most writers rely solely on internal transitions to indicate the movement between subsections, and chances are the clear use of transitions is all your instructor will expect out of you. In longer papers, however, some writers prefer to leave an extra amount of blank area to indicate major sectional breaks while other writers prefer to title these different sections, especially in long papers (ten-thousand words or more) or highly technical articles. Section titles within a paper are called headings and are ordinarily displayed graphically by using larger, thicker, or contrasting fonts. With longer technical documents (like this handbook), there is often a complex system of different-sized headings so that readers can see at a glance the relative importance of the subsequent sections or subsections.

As a general rule, do not use headings within your short (less than five-thousand words), nontechnical essays without guidelines from your instructor.

When you use graphics, tables, or pictures, include white space around them to set them off from the text, and use a clear and consistent means of labeling this material.

Document Design

For a standard college essay, make certain you have

- included a 1-inch margin on all four sides
- double-spaced all text
- used a clear, readable 10- to 12-point font
- incorporated your name and page number as a header on every page
- indented extended quotations 1 inch in from the left margin
- started your Works Cited on a new page
- fixed all awkward line breaks involving dashes or ellipsis points by using hard characters (that is, hard hyphens, hard spaces, and so forth)

15c Understanding Web Documents

The World Wide Web offers users opportunities to search for information (as discussed in sections 6d and 6e, pages 35–39) as well as to publish—that is, to place on a Web server—one's own documents or Web pages. Web servers are computers designed to hold specially formatted Web documents; Web browsers such as Navigator from Netscape and Internet Explorer from Microsoft are software programs created to retrieve and display these documents. At the heart of this arrangement is the recognition that all Web documents contain two radically different kinds of information: (1) the text to be displayed to end users and (2) formatting instructions, intended for Web browsers, about how to display that text. When you view a Web page, you do not view the **source file** with all the distracting formatting instructions visible, but only the presentation of the Web document with all these instructions enacted by the browser. Hence, viewing Web pages is mostly fun, like going to a play, as compared to all the backstage work that goes into creating the pages in the first place.

PLAIN TEXT (OR ASCII) FILES Each word processing document contains the following two sets of information: the text of the document and the formatting information about how that text should be displayed, including such things as margins, fonts, and line spacing. Each word processing program has its own proprietary way of storing all this formatting information in the same file that contains the text file, which is one reason that moving highly formatted text between word processing programs can be difficult. Meanwhile, all word processing programs also give users the option of saving just the text itself, according to a universal standard called ASCII (and pronounced "ASS-key"). ASCII text is a plain text file—lower and uppercase letters, punctuation marks, and the spaces between words all saved according to a universal standard and with all formatting information stripped from the file.

WORD PROCESSING AND WEB DOCUMENTS Web texts are ASCII files (plain text files) with all the formatting and other instructions (such as hyperlinks) reintroduced to and interspersed through the file inside angle brackets: ⟨formatting and linking instructions⟩. The system for creating Web documents by introducing formatting and other nontext instructions inside plain text files is called HTML, for Hypertext Markup Language

The source (or HTML) file for a simple Web page, one that is mostly text, will thus be a lot like a simple text file: primarily text with only a handful of different sets of instructions in angled brackets, whereas the source file for a complex Web page, one with lots of graphics, links, columns (or frames), is likely to resemble the solution to an advanced calculus problem.

HOME PAGES Using the Web entails constantly moving, or linking, from one site on the Web to another. The first page that visitors to any Website expect to see is a home page—an overview of the site with introductory information and links to more information. Large institutions like Microsoft Corporation may have thousands of pages at their Website, all introduced by a single home page, whereas many individuals have only a single home page with information about themselves and links to other, favorite places on the Web.

CREATING A HOME PAGE The two basic steps involved in creating a personal home page are generating an HTML document with information about yourself and favorite links (as explained in the next section), and placing that document on a Web server so that others can access it.

CREATING HTML DOCUMENTS There are three basic ways to create an HTML document.

- The manual way requires editing the source file directly, using a word processor or simple text editor to create a plain text (ASCII) file and adding all the necessary, angle-bracketed formatting instructions by hand.

- The semiautomated way, increasingly built into the latest word processors and browsers, involves selecting formatting preferences from a menu and having the program generate the code that produces the desired look in a browser.
- The fully automated way prompts you through a series of fields or questions, usually at a Website, and produces a limited Web page, displaying the personal information and links that you have entered.

VIEWING HTML DOCUMENTS   A Web browser uses the HTTP command to retrieve and then display HTML documents from Web servers throughout the world; or you can use the FILE command to retrieve and display HTML documents that you have stored on a local network, on a disk drive, or even on a floppy disk. In other words, you can practice creating and editing HTML files and then view them with a Web browser without having to move them to a Web server.

If you are creating the HTML file with a word processor, you will have to save the file and switch to your browser in order to view it. Again, when working with HTML, there is a basic distinction (sometimes involving two different programs) between editing a file and viewing it.

VIEWING (AND EDITING) SOURCE FILES   All browsers allow you to see the source file for the Web page you are currently viewing, although, as noted above, the source file for all but the simplest Web pages, will look more like math than English composition.

E TIP   Creating a Home Page

A home page is an HTML document stored on a Web server designed to give Web users an overview of information about the person or group represented by that page; a personal home page gives the world information about yourself. The hardest task in creating a personal Web page is finding a Web server on which to store your page. All private Internet service providers like CompuServe and America Online provide customers with space for storing any number of such pages, as do many (but not all) colleges.

In April 1998, Yahoo! listed about fifty services providing free space for storing Web pages (under Business and Economy:Companies:Internet Services:Web Services:Free Web Pages), with the most experienced of the companies, like Angelfire Communications (www.angelfire.com), providing templates and other automated systems for greatly simplifying the creation of HTML documents as well. Thus, if you have access to the Internet and a Web browser, all you have to do to create a home page is go to a location like Angelfire and follow the simple, on-screen instructions.

Sentences
and Words

16 Effective Sentences

Effective sentence structure and word choice can help you improve the overall style of your sentences and communicate your meaning clearly. Keep in mind, however, that the purpose of your writing task and the specific focus of each paragraph should affect your choice of words and the structure of your sentences. One good rule to keep in mind is that, in general, English sentences work like relay teams in track: they perform best with the strongest material at the end. For example, if you are assigned an essay on study habits, you should write: "So that you can be admitted into the college of your choice, study hard." On the other hand, if your essay focuses on getting into the college of your choice, you should write: "Study hard so you will be admitted into the college of your choice."

16a Active and Passive Voices

In the active voice, the subject acts; in the passive voice, the subject is acted upon. Use active verbs unless you have a reason to do otherwise. Reserve the passive for specific purposes: to de-emphasize the agent or doer of the action or to create greater coherence between sentences.

ACTIVE VOICE   When possible, use the active voice, with subjects acting on objects.

▶ The judge dismissed the charges against the students.

The subject of the sentence, "judge" is doing the acting.

PASSIVE VOICE   Passive verbs are constructed by combining a form of *to be* and the past-participle form of the verb. When converting a sentence from passive to active, ask yourself who or what acted, and then use your answer as the subject of the sentence. Consider the following:

▶ The charges against one of the students were dismissed by the judge.

To determine how to transform this sentence, ask, "Who dismissed the charges?" Your answer produces the following active sentence: "The judge dismissed the charges against one of the students."

Sometimes you may *choose* to use the passive voice. You may want to draw attention to or away from the subject.

▶ Millions died in the Auschwitz concentration camp. They were remembered by survivors during a recent memorial service.

The first sentence in the above example focuses on "millions" who died and is in the active voice. The second sentence, which is in the passive voice, begins with "they"—a pronoun reference to "millions"—and links the second sentence with the first. In this case, using the passive helps the writer create coherence between sentences.

16b Parallel Construction

Use parallel construction to show the relationships among similar ideas. In the following sentences, the balance of elements heightens the effect of the ideas being conveyed.

▶ Do not ask what your country can do for you. Ask what you can do for your country.

▶ A nation of the people, for the people, and by the people shall not perish from the earth.

Avoid **faulty parallelism**—the failure to put similar items into similar grammatical structures. The writer should revise the following sentences to create parallel structure.

▶ To raise extra revenue, colleges often write grants, conduct fund-raising drives, and alumni _∧ *solicit contributions from* are often asked to contribute.

▶ Some of my hobbies are track, *running* _∧ traveling, and playing volleyball.

| CHECKLIST 12 | Use Parallel Sentence Structure |

- Use repetition effectively.

  ► Give me liberty or give me death.

- Make sure all items in a series are presented in the same grammatical form.

  ► People select foreign cars for their value, ~~they perform well,~~ *their performance* and their style.

- Use coordinating conjunctions (*and*, *but*, *for*, *nor*, *or*, *so*, *yet*) to link and balance sentence elements. The sentence logic and your purpose as a writer should determine your choice of connecting words.

  ► The federal government is giving more power to states and local municipalities *and* taking away power from national agencies.

  And signals an additive relationship and indicates that you see both actions as equally important.

  ► The federal government is giving more power to states, *but* it is taking away money from social services agencies nationally.

  But signals a trade-off.

- Use pairs of correlative conjunctions (*either . . . or; neither . . . nor; not only . . . but also*) to link clauses.

  ► *Neither* my mother *nor* my brother would help me paint my apartment.

16c Coordination and Subordination

Use coordination and subordination to help your reader understand the relationship between ideas in your writing. Coordination refers to the use of coordinate conjunctions (*and, but, for, nor, or, so, yet*) to link parts of sentences. Subordination refers to placing ideas of lesser importance in subordinate (dependent) clauses and placing more important ideas in the main clause.

By deciding which ideas should be subordinated and then selecting the approriate subordinating conjunctions—the words that connect the ideas—you can help readers understand how different ideas relate to one another. Subordinating conjunctions such as the following are used in subordination: *after, although, as, as if, as though, because, before, even though, if, since, so that, than, that, though, unless, until, when, where, whereas, while*.

Although subordination can strengthen your writing, excessive subordination can ruin it. If your sentences go on and on, try shortening them by combining sentences or by deleting unnecessary uses of *that* and *which*.

Use subordinate clauses carefully, making sure that you express ideas or concepts appropriately.

▶ They stopped for lunch and spent time talking.

In the above example, the clauses express concepts that match; therefore, coordination is effective. In the example below, the clauses in the unrevised sentence do not appear to match. The subordinate conjunction *after* gives the reader an indication of the relationship between the clauses in this sentence.

▶ They went shopping, and then they talked about the current state of the economy in Japan and Korea.

REVISED   After they went shopping, they talked about the current state of the economy in Japan and Korea.

If your writing has many short, choppy sentences, you may need to combine some of those sentences, using either coordination or subordination. By selecting an appropriate subordinator, you have a chance to reconsider your meaning in the sentences, and your revision may be significantly different from your original sentence.

▶ The World Wide Web has attracted many kinds of people. It attracts small business owners. Students use it, too. Government agencies provide access to their forms.

REVISED   Because the World Wide Web is so versatile, it has attracted a range of people, including small business owners, students, and government officials.

16d Wordy Sentences

Wordy sentences can obscure your meaning. Aim for clear, direct sentences so readers can follow your ideas.

1. Substitute appositives (words that mean the same thing as the word to which they refer) for clauses beginning with *who* or *which*.

CHECKLIST
13   **Use Coordination and Subordination Effectively**

- Combine equally important short sentences by cutting unnecessary words and by adding needed words and appropriate coordinating conjunctions.

  ▶ Passengers can visit the island at their leisure. If they want, they can remain on board.

  REVISED   Passengers can either visit the island at their leisure or remain on board.

- Reduce less important sentences to phrases or dependent clauses, and combine them with the main clause by using subordinating conjunctions.

  ▶ I worked on the project all night long. But I knew our group would fail.

  REVISED   I worked on the project all night long even though I knew our group would fail.

- Remove unnecessary, repetitive words between sentences.

  ▶ Beekeepers use a centrifuge. The centrifuge is used to extract honey that comes from a comb.

  REVISED   Beekeepers use centrifuges to extract honey that comes from combs.

- Reduce less important sentences or clauses to phrases, using *-ing* or *-ed* words at the beginning or end of a sentence.

  ▶ She has become bored by routine tax-law work. She hopes to become a defense attorney.

  REVISED   Bored by routine tax law, she hopes to become a defense attorney.

  ▶ Mr. Stevens, ~~who was~~ my former neighbor, won his lawsuit.

2. Delete **expletives** (words such as *it is, here is,* and *there is* that are added to a sentence without adding to the meaning of the sentence).

▶ ~~There is a~~ chat area on the Web called Study Hall ~~that~~ *A*

encourages students to talk with one another about
college courses.

3. Use modifiers instead of prepositional and verbal
   phrases.
   ▶ He carries a briefcase ~~made out of leather~~. *leather*

   ▶ He carries a briefcase ~~made out of leather that is weather-beaten~~. *weather-beaten leather*

   Note: Compound modifiers (modifiers made up of
   more than one word, such as "weather-beaten" in the
   example above) are often hyphenated.
4. Eliminate unnecessary words, choosing simple one-
   word expressions rather than longer phrases (see Checklist 14, below).
   ▶ The company is taking applications ~~at this point in time~~. *now*

16e Sentence Variety

Different situations call for different kinds of sentences. News
stories, for example, usually contain relatively short, simple
sentences, whereas editorials and feature stories include longer,
more complex sentences. In all cases, good writing is characterized by variety in sentence structure. Variety heightens in-

**Replace Wordy Expressions
with One-Word Substitutes**

CHECKLIST
14

INSTEAD OF	USE
at this point in time	now
because of the fact that	because
be of the opinion that	think
during the same time that	when
has the ability	can
in spite of the fact that	although
in today's world	today
red in color	red
until such time as	until

terest and allows writers to create an effect that is well suited to the meaning of their text. Consider the following sentences

▶ Another border patrol agent was fired at today by several suspected drug dealers. The suspects escaped.

The second, short sentence of this news report emphasizes that the suspects got away.

▶ Instead of devoting so much attention to protecting the rights of illegal immigrants, we need to consider the dangers being faced daily by the border patrol agents, many of whom are new to this area and far away from family and relatives. Border patrol agents work long hours, protect our downtown streets, and return the next day to face the same dangers all over again. We appreciate their hard work and complement them for their heroic effort. Their efforts this past year have reduced illegal immigration by more than 50% over previous years. They deserve our praise and our support.

The variety in this example, from an editorial, illustrates that well-crafted, long sentences are often easier to follow than shorter sentences, for they demonstrate clear relationships between ideas.

ONLINE TIP A Personal Library of Effective Sentence Patterns

Keep an eye out for particularly well-crafted sentences. When you see them, jot them down and store them in a separate file. While drafting or revising an assignment, refer to the file, and consider imitating sentences that might help you to communicate your thoughts better. See ⟨http://www.wwnorton.com/WE⟩ for a start-up collection of effective sentences.

---

17 Errors in Sentence Wording

17a Misplaced Modifiers

Modifiers are words, phrases, or clauses that describe other words, phrases, or clauses. Modifiers are misplaced if readers are unable to determine what the modifiers describe or explain. To correct a sentence with a misplaced modifier, either move the modifier to a new position or rewrite the sentence.

▶ Marching across the field, the fight song rang out for all to hear.
the band played

The band, not the fight song, is doing the marching.

a business person must spend
at
▶ To be successful ~~in business,~~ long hours ~~of~~ work ~~are required.~~
                          ∧   ∧

Placing the words "long hours" next to "business" implies that long hours—not a person, are doing the working.

While walking home,
▶ Randall found a twenty-dollar bill ~~walking home.~~
  ∧

Randall, not the twenty-dollar bill, was walking home.

MISPLACED LIMITING MODIFIERS Limiting modifiers are words that restrict or limit the meaning of the word or word group they modify. Place limiting modifiers *almost*, *even*, *exactly*, *hardly*, *just*, *merely*, *nearly*, *only*, *scarcely*, and *simply* in front of the word or words you wish to modify. Be sure to create the precise effect you want to have on your reader.

▶ We must *only* go as far as the next town.

The writer is saying that going to the next town is all that we've got to do. The focus is on what has to be done—only going as far as the next town.

▶ We must go *only* as far as the next town.

The writer is focusing on how far we have to go—only to the next town.

▶ The instructor did not *even* call me once.

The writer is focusing on the fact that the instructor not only didn't do other things, he/she didn't even call her.

▶ The instructor did not call me *even* once.

The writer focuses only on the act of calling, noting that the instructor didn't do it even one time.

SQUINTING MODIFIERS A modifier that could refer to the preceding or following words is said to squint. Be sure to place modifiers where the reference is clear. Try moving phrases around so that your meaning is unambiguous.

Before noon, he
▶ ~~He~~ said ~~before noon~~ he'd be here.
  ∧

In the unrevised sentence above, "before noon" could refer to either "He said" or "he'd be here."

DANGLING MODIFIERS Modifiers are said to be dangling when they fail to modify logically any word or words in a sentence. To correct a dangling modifier, ask who or what is responsible for the action described in the opening word group. Immediately after the -*ing* word group, name that person or thing. You may need to rewrite the sentence.

▶ Before going on vacation, the bills ~~need to be paid~~.
  I need to pay ^

▶ After cutting the grass, the garden ~~was weeded~~.
  I weeded ^

▶ ~~Traveling~~ for four weeks, ~~returning~~ to work ~~was a burden~~.
  After traveling ^ *he found it difficult to return*

17b Split Infinitives

An **infinitive** consists of *to* and a verb or verb phrase—for example, *to write*, *to swim well*, *to act quickly*. An infinitive is said to be **split** when a word or words appear between its two parts, as in *to gladly serve*. Infinitives can be split in informal writing, but in college writing and other more formal situations, reword sentences that contain split infinitives. Check with your professor or your employer if you want to be sure of expectations.

▶ To ~~properly~~ care for your plants, you need to repot them
  properly ^
  regularly.

"Properly" modifies the infinitive "to care."

17c Shifts in Construction

Some sentence problems seem accidental and are thus hard to label. This section covers errors that result when a writer inadvertently makes any shift: a shift away from topics in the subject of the sentence; a shift in tense; a shift in pronoun person and number; and a shift from statements to commands or from statements to wishes, often called shifts in mood.

SHIFT FROM SUBJECT TO PREDICATE   When you start an idea in the subject part of a sentence, you must complete that idea—not another idea—in the predicate. To correct sentences that end up differently from the way they started, you may need to reconsider completely the point you want to make.

▶ ~~When I bake~~ cookies relaxes me.
  Baking ^

or

▶ ~~When~~ I bake cookies ~~relaxes me~~.
  I relax when ^

In the first revision, the subject matches the predicate. In the second revision, the predicate completes the sentence structure implied by the subject.

▶ ~~My appointment to~~ Director ~~was~~ the position I wanted.
   $\overset{I\ was\ appointed}{\wedge}$ $\overset{,}{\wedge}$

The revised version makes distinct the two ideas in the sentence: the appointment and the writer's note that she wanted the job.

SHIFT IN TENSE   The verb tense used in a sentence should give readers a clear idea of the *time* of the action described. Be consistent in using verb tense, shifting tenses only as required. An abrupt shift in tense can confuse readers.

▶ Workers who ~~were~~ consulted regularly feel more committed to
   $\overset{are}{\wedge}$

   the company and ~~had~~ a lower rate of absenteeism.
   $\overset{have}{\wedge}$

   or

▶ Workers who ~~were~~ consulted regularly feel more committed to
   $\overset{have\ been}{\wedge}$ $\overset{now}{\wedge}$

   the company and have a lower rate of absenteeism.

The original sentence refers to an action in the past ("workers were consulted"), then switches to the present ("regularly feel"), then moves back to the past "had a lower rate". To revise a sentence with faulty predication, you must clarify your intent as a writer.

As a rule, use the present tense when referring to the actions of literary characters.

▶ Hamlet ~~delayed~~ because he ~~was~~ overwhelmed by the events of
   $\overset{delays}{\wedge}$ $\overset{is}{\wedge}$

   the past few days.

SHIFT IN PRONOUN PERSON AND NUMBER   Pronoun references should be consistent throughout a paper. That is, if you start writing from one point of view, do not shift to another. If you are writing about yourself, then maintain an *I* point of view throughout the paper.

▶ My summer internships gave me the opportunity to observe different business settings. I discovered that I like working for a faster-paced company, one in which workers rarely leave before 6 P.M.

If you are addressing the reader directly, maintain a "your" point of view.

> ► Go to the first stop sign, then turn right. After traveling for three blocks, watch for a bridge.

If you start writing a paper in the third person (using pronouns such as *he, she, it,* or *they* and synonyms such as *a person, a platypus, students,* and *tourists*), a shift to *I* may be appropriate, but not a shift to *you.*

> ► Characters in each of these stories were driven to express their
>
>   creativity. ~~You~~ can't help but wonder whether the woman in
>
>   "The Yellow Wallpaper" would have recovered if she had been
>
>   allowed to write.

Note: Although many teachers now recognize that *I* and *you* are used in many writing situations, including some academic publications, some teachers still oppose the use of *I* or *you* in college papers. Remember that it is possible, and often better, to state your opinions without using *I.* If you are uncertain about using *I* or *you,* check with your instructor.

> ► ~~I personally feel that affirmative~~ Affirmative action is not fair to minorities.

(In an opinion essay, your readers recognize that the statements you make are your "personal feelings." You do not have to use the words "I personally feel" or "I think.")

SHIFT FROM STATEMENTS TO COMMANDS (SHIFT IN MOOD)

A shift in mood refers to a shift in the approach to a topic. In the indicative mood, ideas are expressed matter-of-factly.

> ► Your room needs to be cleaned.

The imperative mood is characterized by commands or requests.

> ► Clean your room.

The subjunctive mood refers to wishes or statements contrary to fact.

> ► If I were going to clean my room, I would have done it already.

Avoid abrupt shifts from statements to commands. If a shift is necessary, signal the change to your readers. Alternately, consider more extensive revision.

▶ Next, I will explain how to format a disk. First, insert the disk into the disk drive.

The above shift from indicative to imperative is acceptable. The writer eliminates the *I* point of view and prepares the reader to expect technical directions in list format.

SHIFT FROM DIRECT TO INDIRECT DISCOURSE   Direct discourse consists of the actual words of a speaker, with quotation marks around the words. Indirect discourse is a translation or restatement of what the speaker said; no quotation marks are used unless a portion of the original words are included in the restatement. Indirect discourse usually begins with something like "He said that . . ." and is followed by a restatement of the speaker's words.

DIRECT DISCOURSE	President Garcia stated, "I want to see many more low-income students—especially more Hispanic students from the Rio Grande Valley—go to college."
INDIRECT DISCOURSE	President Garcia said that she wanted more low-income students to go to college.

You may not have room to paraphrase the complete meaning, but be especially careful to report the main idea.

18 Errors in Punctuating Sentences

Sentences begin with a capital letter and end with an end punctuation mark, most often a period. Students frequently have difficulty punctuating sentences—using end punctuation when there is no complete sentence (creating a fragment) or punctuating two or more complete sentences as if they were a single sentence (run-on sentence or comma splice).

18a Fragments

A sentence is a group of words that contains a subject and a finite verb (a verb with tense) and that expresses a complete thought. A sentence fragment is a group of words that is punctuated like a sentence (that is, it begins with a capital letter and ends with end punctuation) but lacks one or more of the elements of a sentence. Although on occasion you might use a fragment intentionally for stylistic effect, it is best to avoid fragments in academic writing.

▶ Although he is a successful businessman. _he wants to become a teacher_

Be careful not to mistake "although" for "however." "However he is a successful businessman" *is* a complete sentence.

▶ Whatever you think. _I'll do whatever_

In casual conversation, "Whatever you think" is acceptable. It is not acceptable, however, in academic writing.

CHECKLIST 15 **Add Needed Words to Fragments**

- Supply the missing subject.

  ▶ Went downtown. _She went_

- Supply the missing subject and the correct finite verb.

  ▶ Having known her for twenty years. _I have_

- Attach the fragment to an independent clause.

  ▶ Although she wants to go to college.

  REVISED Although she wants to go to college, she plans to work for a year before she enrolls.

18b Comma Splices and Run-On Sentences

A comma splice occurs when independent clauses are joined with a comma rather than with a semicolon or a conjunction (and another clause), or severed with a period. (For more on using semicolons, see pages 159–60.)

▶ The acting was competent; the direction was faulty.

Run-on (or fused) sentences are aptly labeled. They run on and on with neither the necessary punctuation to separate them nor the appropriate conjunctions to join them. Sometimes writers create run-on sentences accidentally because they want to link closely related ideas.

▶ I sang softly it still scared the dog. _, but_

Repair Comma Splices and Run-On Sentences

● Join the independent parts on both sides of the comma splice with a semicolon.

 ▶ I work all day; I exercise in the evening.

● Use subordination to show a clearer relationship between the two independent clauses. Use a conjunction to connect the two independent clauses, thus turning one of them into a dependent clause. Make as many revisions to the sentence as you care to make.

 ▶ Because I sit at a desk all day, I enjoy exercising in the evening.

● End the first sentence with a period. Make the second sentence into a freestanding one. *Note:* Frequently, you must do more than merely insert the punctuation; you may have to revise more extensively if the revised sentences mean more effective paragraph structure.

 ▶ I work all day long. I rush to the gym to exercise in the evening.

19 Effective Word Choice

Adapting your language—your choice of words—to the audience, occasion, and purpose of your papers will help you to communicate your meaning more clearly to readers.

19a Formal and Informal Words

Different words and expressions are appropriate for different occasions. Just as you would not wear cut-offs to a wedding, you would not describe a literary figure as "the pits" in a paper; to do this would be inappropriately informal.

If you are unsure of the audience and purpose of your writing, maintain a general level of usage. If you know the audience and purpose, then adapt your usage to the context. Keep in mind, however, that words that are either too formal or too casual tend to draw attention to themselves and thus should serve some constructive purpose when used.

If you are writing a letter of application, you might end by using words such as the following:

 ▶ If you have any questions, please do not hesitate to call.

You would not write a sentence such as this one:

▶ It would be cool if you'd give me a buzz.

Similarly, in a history paper, the following would be inappropriate:

▶ General Lee was a regular kind of guy.

Instead, you might write this:

▶ General Lee was an unassuming kind of leader, one who mixed easily with his troops.

The words "regular kind of guy" are too casual for the purpose of this assignment; The words "unassuming kind of leader" state the same idea in more appropriate words.

Consider the circumstances in which you might use each of the following words or phrases:

FORMAL	INFORMAL
celebration	party
momentous	important
deceased	dead
position	job
wish to	would like to
onerous	difficult
beneficent	generous
misfortune	bad luck

19b Specific and General Words

Specific words provide precise, sensory, or concrete details. General words convey inexact, intangible, and often abstract concepts. You often want to use general terms in the beginning of a paragraph. Be sure to follow up with sentences that give the reader a more specific notion of what you are talking about.

Some writing tasks require more use of abstractions than others. The degree of specificity required depends on your topic and your focus.

▶ The president's knowledge of domestic issues is superior to his understanding of foreign policy. He has been more successful with welfare reform, for example, than with peace in the Middle East.

In this context, "Domestic issues" and "foreign policy" are used in a general sense in the first sentence. The writer then elabo

rates by clarifying specific kinds ...
"peace in the Middle East") refer...
terms in the earlier sentence.

Choose Precise Words

INSTEAD OF	CONSIDER
a *good* movie	a *suspenseful, terrifying, lighthearte...*
a *nice* smile	a *winning, angelic, purposeful* smile
someone *I know*	a *friend, an acquaintance, a colleague, a ...* worker
walked	*paced, strutted, strolled, marched*

19c Figurative Language

Figurative language refers to similes, metaphors, and other rhetorical uses of language. Although effective figurative language can help readers visualize your meaning, ineffective figurative language can ruin the intended effect. In general, state ideas in your own words, and avoid clichés and trite expressions that add nothing distinctive to your meaning. *Note:* A particular danger in using trite expressions is the **mixed metaphor**, a situation that occurs when a writer unknowingly allows two or more metaphoric images to clash.

▶ If you build your plans on sand, they may collapse.

REVISED   If you don't test the new menu design with users, you can expect complaints.

In the revision, the specific situation is clearly stated in the sentence. In the original, it is not clear what "plans" might "collapse."

▶ Think of your computer screen as a desktop.

The desktop metaphor has helped people understand the concept of keeping files on the top level of the computer screen.

▶ We won by ~~leaps and bounds~~.
  20 points
  ∧

19d Biased Language

You are expected to use language that avoids bias of any kind. In particular, avoid gender, ethnic, and age bias.

Avoiding Biased Language

Use gender-neutral terms: *reporter* rather than *newsman*; *to staff* rather than *to man*; *representative* rather than *congressman*.

- Avoid sexist stereotyping.

  ► The ~~wives~~ [*spouses*] will have an opportunity to tour the city during the conference.

- Use the plural to avoid the awkward use of *he* or *she* (see page 140).

  ► ~~A~~ [*Writers*] ~~writer~~ usually revises ~~his or her~~ [*their*] work several times.

- Avoid age bias.

  ► The ~~kids~~ [*young people*] can sit at the extra table.

  ► ~~Old~~ [*Senior*] professors are often more current in their field than their younger colleagues.

- Avoid terms of ethnic bias.

  ► Many ~~Orientals~~ [*Asians*] live in the outer boroughs.

- Use gender-neutral, nonsexist words.

  ► The ~~stewardess~~ [*flight attendant*] served the coach passengers a light snack.

  ► The department ~~chairman~~ [*head*] called a meeting.

- Avoid sexist stereotyping.

  ► If there is a doctor in the house, will he [*or she*] please step forward?

- Use terms that show respect for people's ethnic backgrounds.

  ► My friend is ~~Oriental~~ [*Asian*].

  Or use specific nationality, such as Chinese or Japanese.

  ► Some of the students at the university are Mexican; most of them, however, are Mexican American.

  The term *Mexican* should be used only for individuals who are Mexican nationals.

  ► The black students on many college campuses are not all African Americans. Some blacks are African American; some rates by clarifying specific kinds of issues ("welfare reform" and "peace in the Middle East") referred to by the more general terms in the earlier sentence.

CHECKLIST 17

Choose Precise Words

INSTEAD OF	CONSIDER
a *good* movie	a *suspenseful, terrifying, lighthearted* movie
a *nice* smile	a *winning, angelic, purposeful* smile
someone I know	*a friend, an acquaintance, a colleague, a co-worker*
walked	*paced, strutted, strolled, marched*

19c Figurative Language

Figurative language refers to similes, metaphors, and other rhetorical uses of language. Although effective figurative language can help readers visualize your meaning, ineffective figurative language can ruin the intended effect. In general, state ideas in your own words, and avoid clichés and trite expressions that add nothing distinctive to your meaning. *Note:* A particular danger in using trite expressions is the mixed metaphor, a situation that occurs when a writer unknowingly allows two or more metaphoric images to clash.

► If you build your plans on sand, they may collapse.

REVISED   If you don't test the new menu design with users, you can expect complaints.

In the revision, the specific situation is clearly stated in the sentence. In the original, it is not clear what "plans" might "collapse."

► Think of your computer screen as a desktop.

The desktop metaphor has helped people understand the concept of keeping files on the top level of the computer screen.

► We won by ~~leaps and bounds~~. _20 points_

19d Biased Language

You are expected to use language that avoids bias of any kind. In particular, avoid gender, ethnic, and age bias.

Avoiding Biased Language

- Use gender-neutral terms: *reporter* rather than *newsman; to staff* rather than *to man; representative* rather than *congressman.*
- Avoid sexist stereotyping.
  - ▶ The ~~wives~~ will have an opportunity to tour the city during the conference.

    spouses ^

- Use the plural to avoid the awkward use of *he* or *she* (see page 140).
  - ▶ A ~~writer~~ usually revises ~~his or her~~ work several times.

    Writers ^ *their* ^

- Avoid age bias.
  - ▶ The ~~kids~~ can sit at the extra table.

    young people ^

  - ▶ ~~Old~~ professors are often more current in their field than their younger colleagues.

    Senior ^

- Avoid terms of ethnic bias.
  - ▶ Many ~~Orientals~~ live in the outer boroughs.

    Asians ^

- Use gender-neutral, nonsexist words.
  - ▶ The ~~stewardess~~ served the coach passengers a light snack.

    flight attendant ^

  - ▶ The department ~~chairman~~ called a meeting.

    head ^

- Avoid sexist stereotyping.
  - ▶ If there is a doctor in the house, will he please step forward?

    or she ^

- Use terms that show respect for people's ethnic backgrounds
  - ▶ My friend is ~~Oriental~~.

    Asian ^

  Or use specific nationality, such as Chinese or Japanese.

  - ▶ Some of the students at the university are Mexican; most of them, however, are Mexican American.

  The term *Mexican* should be used only for individuals who are Mexican nationals.

  - ▶ The black students on many college campuses are not all African Americans. Some blacks are African American; some are African; and others are Islanders from Haiti, Jamaica, and Antigua.

- Use terms that show respect for people's age.

  ► She is ~~an old lady~~.
    elderly

  ► ~~Kids~~ today are not as willing to read as they were in earlier
    Young people

    times.

  ► Do you ~~girls~~ want to join us for a golf match?
    women

In the latter example, use "women" if you are referring to adults.

20 Usage Glossary

a Use *a* before consonant sounds (*a car, a history, a union*). **an** Use *an* before vowel sounds (*an elk, an X-ray, an herb*).

accept (verb) "to take," "to receive": *I accept the award gladly.* **except** (preposition) "not counting": *Except for the lack of plumbing, the apartment is perfect;* (verb) "to leave out": *Please except that package from the group.*

adapt (verb) "to adjust": *Some people adapt easily to new environments.* **adept** (adjective) "skillful": *She is adept at mastering new tasks.* **adopt** (verb) "to care for as one's own": *He adopts a new image when needed.*

advice (noun) "guidance": *My doctor gave me sound advice.* **advise** (verb) "to recommend," "to inform": *I often advise her on what to wear.*

affect (verb) "to influence": *Technology affects people in different ways.* **effect** (noun) "consequence": *It has both positive and negative effects on job performance;* (verb) "to bring about," "to cause to occur": *Skiing effects a sense of exhilaration.*

aid (noun) "assistance": *Her role is to provide aid to homeless children;* (verb) "to assist": *She aids homeless children.* **aide** (noun) "an assistant": *As an aide, she helps in countless ways.*

allude "to make reference to": *Poets frequently allude to Greek and Roman myths.* **elude** "to avoid capture": *Some poems elude interpretation.*

allusion "indirect reference": *In his footnotes, Eliot explains the allusions in "The Waste Land" to readers.* **illusion** "false appearance": *Her weight loss is an illusion.*

a lot (always two words) "many": *She has a lot of energy.* alot Incorrect spelling of *a lot.*

all ready "everyone prepared": *The students are all ready to ex plore the Internet.* already "previously": *Already, the teacher ha assigned the first two chapters.*

all right (always two words) "satisfactory," "certainly": *It is al right to admit that you are wrong.* alright Incorrect spelling o *all right.*

all together "everyone in one place": *When we put our resource. all together, we discovered that we had more than we needed to cove our expenses.* altogether "completely": *You have an altogethe different reading list.*

altar (noun) "place of worship": *The altar was decorated with flowers.* alter (verb) "to change": *The flowers altered the usua appearance of the church.*

among "shared by a group" (usually three or more): *They are among the ten best athletes in the school.* between "shared by individuals" (usually two): *Tara sat between Julia and Peter.*

amount (noun) "quantity of something that cannot be counted": *The amount of money needed to fund the project is stag gering.* (verb) "to equal": *It doesn't amount to much.* number (noun) "quantity of something that can be counted": *The num ber of students required for state funding is 750;* (verb) "to in clude," "to assign a number to": *The chorus numbers twenty.*

anxious "nervous, worried": *I am anxious about my grades* eager "characterized by enthusiastic interest": *I am eager to go on vacation.*

any more "no more": *We don't want to buy any more property* anymore "any longer": *We don't live here anymore.*

anyone "any person": *Did anyone come?* any one "any mem ber of a group": *Any one of you would be welcome.*

anyways Nonstandard for *anyway.*

anywheres Nonstandard for *anywhere.*

appraise "to calculate value": *The teacher appraises students' abil ities at midterm.* apprise "to inform": *He apprises them of their strengths and weaknesses.*

as (conjunction) "in the way that": *The computer didn't work a. the instructions said it would.* like (preposition) "similar to":

would prefer a computer like Anna's. Do not use *like* in place of *as* or *as if* in formal writing: *They acted as if they were drunk.*

ascent (noun) "rising," "advancement": *The ascent of the rocket into space was swift.* assent (verb) "to agree": *I assent to the compromise;* (noun) "agreement": *After winning the school board's assent, schools began to include Darwinism in the curriculum.*

assistance (noun) "aid": *Work-study students provide assistance in the library.* assistants (plural noun) "helpers": *The librarian always requests additional student assistants.*

bad (adjective) "not good," "sick," "sorry": *This is a bad situation.* badly (adverb) "not well": *We have performed badly.*

bare (adjective) "naked": *I like to walk around with bare feet;* (verb) "to expose": *I bared my soul to the poetry of the moment.* bear (noun) "animal": *The polar bear is an arctic resident;* (verb) "to carry," "to tolerate": *I cannot bear to listen to that music.*

bazaar (noun) "marketplace or fair for the sale of goods": *On our vacation to Mexico, we visited several local bazaars.* bizarre (adjective) "strange": *It was bizarre to run into our neighbors in Mexico.*

because of See *due to/because of.*

beside (preposition) "next to": *We sat beside the president of the company.* besides (preposition) "in addition to," "except": *Besides the members' spouses, we were the only visitors invited;* (adverb) "moreover," "also": *I don't want to go to class; besides, I love the park.*

between See *among/between.*

bring "to move an object toward something": *Bring your roommate to the party.* take "to move an object away from something": *When you exit the train, take your belongings.*

can "to be able to do something": *With practice, you can learn the difference between* can *and* may. may "to ask for or be granted permission": *You may not use* can *in this sentence.*

capital "city in which the seat of government is located": *Santa Fe is the capital of New Mexico;* (noun) "possessions and their value": *If we want more capital, we'll have to raise more money.* capitol "the building that houses the legislature": *In Santa Fe, the capitol is shaped like a Zia sun symbol.*

censer (noun) "incense burner": *The censer gave off a lot of smoke.* censor (verb) "to alter," "to delete": *Many critics would love to censor this artist's work;* (noun) "one who censors": *The censor didn't like my sentence, so he censored it.* censure (noun) "condemnation"; (verb) "to blame," "to condemn": *The student government censured me for making that statement.*

cite (verb) "to acknowledge": *When you quote someone in a paper, be sure you cite the source.* sight (noun) "ability to see," "something that is seen": *Wearing an eight-foot feathered headdress, he was a magnificent sight;* (verb) "to glimpse": *In Memphis last week, Elvis was sighted in the supermarket.* site (noun) "location": *The archeological site exposed several layers of human occupation;* (verb) "to place": *I sited the deer tracks in the forest.*

coarse (adjective) "rough": *The texture of the fabric is coarse.* course (noun) "path," "unit of study": *This is a writing course.*

complement (noun) "that which completes": *The baby had the full complement of fingers and toes;* (verb) "to complete": *The printed book complements the online tutorial.* compliment (noun) "expression of admiration": *The author paid Carol a compliment;* (verb) "to flatter": *The author complimented Carol.*

conscience (noun) "sense of right and wrong": *He reads my stories only because he has a guilty conscience.* conscious (adjective) "aware": *He is not conscious of how others react to him.*

continual "repeatedly," "over and over": *Updating our database is a continual process.* continuous "without interruption": *The continuous rivalry between the two of them was harmful.*

could care less Nonstandard for *couldn't care less.*

could of Nonstandard for *could have.*

council (noun) "advisory or legislative body": *The council of elders debated my future.* counsel (noun) "advice": *Her counsel was useful;* (verb) "to give advice": *In the end, they counseled me wisely.*

criteria (plural of criterion) "standard for judgment": *The criteria for choosing the winner were varied.*

data (plural of datum) "facts": *The data are here in this research report.*

defer "to delay," "to yield": *I defer to your judgment.* differ "to disagree," "to be unlike": *I beg to differ with you.*

deference "respect," "consideration": *We turned the music down in deference to those who wanted to sleep.* difference "being unlike": *You and I have a difference of opinion.* diffidence "shyness": *His diffidence accounts for his lack of a social life.*

desert (noun) "dry, barren place": *The heat of the desert was fierce;* (verb) "to leave": *I will not desert my friends.* dessert (noun) "sweet course at the end of a meal": *Dessert is my favorite part of any meal.*

device (noun) "plan," "piece of equipment": *A mouse is a device used to move a pointer in a computer program.* devise (verb) "to think up": *Whoever devised the mouse had a great idea.*

different from *Different from* is preferred to *different than: His attitude toward studying is different from mine.* different than Use *different than* when a construction using *different from* is wordy: *I am a different person than I was two years ago.*

due to "resulting from": *The bags under my eyes are due to stress.* because of "as the result of": *My grade in the class dropped because of this assignment.*

eager See *anxious/eager.*

effect See *affect/effect.*

elude See *allude/elude.*

eminent "prominent," "important": *The professor was eminent in the field.* immanent "operating within reality," "inherent": *Knowing which word to use is not an immanent skill—it must be learned.* imminent "about to happen": *The test is imminent.*

enthused Use *enthusiastic: The grammarian was enthusiastic when he praised me for never using* enthused.

envelop (verb) "to enclose completely": *The mist will envelop us as soon as we enter the rain forest.* envelope (noun) "wrapper, usually for a letter": *Place the invitation in the envelope.*

every one "each individual": *Every one of the athletes was tested for steroid use.* everyone "all": *Everyone participated in the talent show.*

except See *accept/except.*

farther "at a greater distance": *Ken's rescue team traveled farther than my team did to help the victims.* further "to a greater degree": *Ken explained that further travel was necessary to reach those in need of help.*

few, fewer "a limited number of countable items": *A few of us went to the concert.* little, less "a small quantity of an uncountable item": *It will cost less if you make it yourself.*

formally "not casually": *The rules were formally approved by the city council.* formerly "before": *Formerly, there were no guidelines about sorting household trash.*

good (adjective) not to be used in place of the adverb *well*: *This plan is good.* well (adverb): *The plan will work well.*

hanged "killed by hanging": *The victors hanged their enemies.* hung "suspended": *I hung my clothes out to dry.*

hisself Nonstandard for *himself.*

hopefully "filled with hope": *We moved hopefully toward the future.* Do not use *hopefully* to mean "I hope that," "we hope that," and so forth.

human (noun or adjective) "referring to people": *To be fallible is to be human.* humane (adjective) "compassionate": *The humane treatment of animals is uppermost in Kate's mind.*

illusion See *allusion/illusion.*

immanent See *eminent/immanent/imminent.* imminent See *eminent/immanent/imminent.*

imply "to suggest indirectly": *I don't mean to imply that you are wrong.* infer "to draw a conclusion": *You may have inferred from what I said that I love you.*

incidence "rate of occurrence": *The incidence of heart disease among Americans is high.* incidents "occurrences": *Many incidents during the Revolution led to American patriot losses.*

irregardless Nonstandard for *regardless.*

its (possessive pronoun) "belonging to it": *Its colors were iridescent.* it's contraction for *it is: It's a great day.*

kind of/sort of Avoid *kind of* and *sort of* when you mean "somewhat": *The movie was somewhat scary.*

later (adverb) "subsequently": *We'll play with the kitten later.* latter (adjective) "last mentioned": *Of the two stories, I prefer the latter.*

lay (verb + object) "to place something": *He lay the book on the table.* lie (verb + no object) "to assume or be in a reclining position": *He went to his bedroom to lie down.*

lead (verb) "to go before": *If you lead, we will follow;* (noun) "metal," "position at the front": *Anthony Hopkins played the lead.* led past participle of *lead: When you led us yesterday, we followed you.*

less See *few/fewer/little/less.*

lessen (verb) "to decrease": *Your bravery will lessen our fear.* lesson (noun) "something learned by study or experience": *That is the lesson I learned from you.*

liable "obligated, responsible": *The landlord is liable for the roof repairs.* likely "future possibility": *Even if the roof isn't leaking now, it is likely to leak in the future.*

lie See *lay/lie.*

like See *as/like.*

little See *few/fewer/little/less.*

loose (adjective) "not tight": *The bolts on the car door are loose.* lose (verb) "to misplace," "to not win": *If we invest poorly, we might lose our money.*

many "large number of something countable": *Many of our investments will pay off.* much "large number of something uncountable": *Much effort was wasted in this endeavor.*

may See *can/may.*

may be (verb) "might be": *I may be getting better.* maybe (adverb) "perhaps": *Maybe we should open a savings account.*

may of Nonstandard for *may have.*

media Plural of *medium: Computers, newspapers, and TV are communications media. Media* has also come to have a singular sense in speech. Formally, use the plural.

might of Nonstandard for *might have.*

much See *many/much.*

must of Nonstandard for *must have.*

nowheres Nonstandard for *nowhere.*

number See *amount/number.*

number of *Number of* should be followed by a plural noun: *a number of options.*

off of *Of* is unnecessary: *Get off the road!*

passed (verb) past tense of *pass: Roaring down the road, he passed me.* past (adjective) "previous": *His past exploits are legendary.*

patience (noun) "ability to wait": *Have some patience.* patient (adjective) "calm": *Be patient;* (noun) "someone receiving medical treatment": *I was his only patient.*

persecute "to harrass": *He felt persecuted by her attentions.* prosecute "to bring to trial": *She was prosecuted for grand larceny.*

personal (adjective) "relating to an individual," "private": *I don't care to share details of my personal life.* personnel (noun) "employees": *The director of personnel takes all new employees to lunch.*

phenomena Plural of *phenomenon,* "observable facts or events": *Like other astronomical phenomena, the eclipse can be easily explained.*

plus Do not use *plus* to join independent clauses; use *moreover* or *in addition to: Your salary in addition to mine will cover our expenses.*

precede "to come before": *She preceded me into the house.* proceed "to go forward," "to continue": *Please, proceed carefully into the room.*

prescribe "to order treatment": *The doctor will prescribe a medicine to relieve the pain.* proscribe "to forbid": *Smoking is proscribed here.*

principal (noun) "chief person," "capital sum": *We may earn no interest, but we won't lose the principal;* (adjective) "most important": *The book's principal effect was to change my viewpoint on the economics of ecology.* principle (noun) "rule," "fundamental law": *Tornadoes are based upon physical principles.*

raise (verb + object) "to lift," "to grow": *She raised her arms heavenward;* (noun) "increase in salary." rise (verb + no object) "to get up": *Hot air balloons, however, rise more slowly;* (noun) "ascent," "hilltop": *The rise in temperature was deadly.*

respectfully "with respect": *We behave respectfully around him.* respectively "in the order named": *We saw Kurt, Marian, and Diane, respectively, enter the building.*

right (adjective) "correct": *Roberta was the right woman for the job;* (noun) "something allowed," "location of the right side," "conservative position": *It is their right as Americans.* rite (noun) "ceremony": *For New Yorkers, the first Yankees game is a rite of passage.*

sensual "pleasing to the senses, especially sexual": *Don Juan was addicted to sensual experiences.* sensuous "pleasing to the senses, particularly with regard to the arts": *The poet's use of sensuous detail helped us see, smell, and taste the food.*

set (verb + object) "to place something": *I set the dish on the table.* sit (verb + no object) "to be in or assume a sitting position": *I will sit here and eat my dinner.*

should of Nonstandard for *should have.*

sight See *cite/sight/site.*

site See *cite/sight/site.*

some time (adjective + noun) "span of time": *We have some time before the test begins.* sometime (adverb) "at an unspecified time": *I will probably feel nervous about it sometime soon.* sometimes (adverb) "now and then," "occasionally": *Sometimes I'm funny that way.*

somewheres Nonstandard for *somewhere.*

sort of See *kind of/sort of.*

stationary (adjective) "not moving": *When the wind died, the sailboat was stationary.* stationery (noun) "letter paper": *The captain took out her stationery and wrote a letter to her husband.*

statue "sculpture": *The* Venus de Milo *is a famous statue.* stature "height," "status": *The sculptor had great stature among his peers.* statute "law": *The town has many outdated statutes in its civil code.*

suppose to Incorrect spelling of *supposed to.*

take See *bring/take.*

than (conjunction) used in comparisons: *Learning to sail was easier than learning to windsurf.* then (adverb) "at that time," "besides": *Then I ran the boat aground.*

that Use *that* for essential clauses: *The handbook that we use for English is written by Rodrigues and Tuman.* which Use *which* for nonessential clauses: *The text, which was written by Rodrigues and Tuman, includes suggestions for using a word processor.*

their (pronoun) "belonging to them": *Their values are not my values.* there (adverb) "in that place": *"The mouse is over there!"*

he screamed; (expletive) used to introduce a sentence or clause: *There are some values I accept.* they're contraction for *they are:* *They're probably more comfortable than I am.*

theirselves Nonstandard for *themselves*.

thorough (adjective) "exhaustive": *His review of my essay was thorough.* through (preposition) "in and then out": *He did not drive through it with his car;* (adverb) "completely," "finished": *I was soaked through.*

to (preposition) "toward": *I am going to school.* too (adverb) "in addition," "excessively": *I am going to the store, too.* two (noun) "one more than one": *I am going to two places.*

try and Nonstandard for *try to*.

unique "one of a kind": *Among actors, Jimmy Stewart is unique.*

use to Nonstandard for *used to*.

wear (verb) "to bear or carry on the person," "to cause to degenerate by use": *You can wear what you want.* were (verb) past tense of *be: You were raised to do the right thing.* where (adverb or conjunction) "in that place": *You can go where you want.*

weather (noun) "atmosphere": *The weather outside is frightful.* whether (conjunction) "if": *I don't know whether it will ever be delightful.*

well See *good/well*.

which See *that/which*.

which/who Do not use *which* to refer to people; use *who: She is the person who helped me the most.*

who Use *who* for subjects and subject complements: *I will check to see who is at the door.* whom Use *whom* for objects: *I am the person whom she helped.*

who's Contraction of *who is: Who's this sweating at the table?* whose (pronoun) possessive form of *who: He's the person whose tongue is burning from the chili peppers.*

would of Nonstandard for *would have*.

your (pronoun) "belonging to you": *Your cleverness amazes me.* you're Contraction for *you are: You're a clever person.*

Grammar

21 Verbs

Verbs express action or show a state of existence (*be* verbs) by linking the subject to the rest of the sentence. Sentences must have at least one verb, but they can have several. Verbs indicate the **tense** or time an action or state of existence occurred, is occurring, or will occur.

▶ The top salesperson *sold* more than fifty cars last month. [action in the past]

▶ The book *is available* in the bookstore at the beginning of the term. [state of being in the present]

Verbs often use auxiliary or helping words such as *had, can, might, will,* or *would* to form different tenses.

▶ The book *will be* available in June. [future]

▶ The ship *might have been* seaworthy. [conditional]

21a Subject-Verb Agreement

The subject and verb in a sentence or clause must **agree** or match. If the subject is singular, the verb must be singular; if the subject is plural, the verb must be plural. If the subject is in the **first person** (*I, we*), the verb must be in the first person (*I am, we are*). The same rule holds true for subjects in the **second person** or **third person** (*you are; he/she/it is, they are*).

	SINGULAR	PLURAL
FIRST PERSON	I sing	we sing
SECOND PERSON	you sing	you sing
THIRD PERSON	he/she/it sings	they sing

INTERVENING WORDS Sometimes a word or phrase comes between the subject and the verb. Ignore that word or phrase when locating the subject and verb, making sure that the verb agrees with the subject.

► My *brother*, along with our friends, *is* looking forward to this weekend.

► One of my friends ~~are~~ is graduating.

Hint: To test subject-verb agreement, mentally recite the sentence *without* the intervening words. That is, replace the complete subject "one of my friends is graduating" with "one is graduating."

COMPOUND SUBJECTS JOINED BY *AND* When the parts of a subject are joined by *and*, the verb is usually plural.

► Captain Janeway and three other officers *were* honored.

► The coach and the quarterback *understand* what teamwork means.

The exception occurs when the subject is a single item, like a food dish (for example, *strawberries and cream*), formed by joining together two items.

► Red beans and rice *is* a popular dish in Louisiana.

Hint: To make subject-and-verb agreement easier, try substituting a pronoun for the compound subject. For instance, in the football example, above, substituting "they" for the compound subject "the coach and the quarterback" results in "they understand."

COMPOUND SUBJECT JOINED BY *OR* OR *NOR* When parts of a subject are joined by *or* or *nor*, the verb agrees with the closer noun.

► Neither my mother nor my other relatives ~~is~~ are happy with the decision.

► Either the administrators or the union ~~are~~ is to blame.

INDEFINITE PRONOUNS AS SUBJECTS Indefinite pronouns refer to nonspecific individuals (*anybody, anyone, each, either, everybody, everyone, everything, neither, none, no one, somebody, someone, something*) and, hence, seem to be plural. However, most are singular.

► Everyone *likes* English.

► None of us *has* classes today.

Note: There is a tendency to use the plural possessive-pronoun form *their* to refer to indefinite pronouns since it conveniently refers to both males and females. Most teachers and editors, however, still expect the standard rule for agreement to be followed—hence, the need for *his or her*, as in "Everyone should turn in his or her final draft." Of course, one could be more concise and say, "Students should turn in their final drafts."

Some indefinite pronouns are always plural (*few, many*).

▶ Many *are called*, but few *are chosen*.

Some indefinite pronouns (*all, any, some*) are either singular or plural, depending on the noun or pronoun to which they refer.

▶ All of the students [plural] *like* English.

▶ All of the water [singular] *is* gone.

COLLECTIVE NOUNS AS SUBJECTS Most collective nouns (nouns that refer to a group) are considered singular.

▶ The *class has selected* her president.

▶ The *group wants* to remain seated.

Numerical collective nouns are either singular or plural, depending on whether the focus of the sentence is on the group or on the individual members of the group.

▶ A *majority* of team members *have* injuries.

▶ A *majority* of team members *has* selected Barbara as captain.

In the first sentence, the focus is on the many team members who have injuries. In the second, the team members in the majority are considered as a unit.

REVERSED SUBJECTS AND VERBS The verb must agree with its grammatical subject even when the subject appears after the verb. When the subject of a sentence is placed after the verb, identifying the subject can be tricky. Remember that expressions such as *there is* and *there are* (expletives) do not contain the subject. (See section 16d, pages 108–9, for a discussion of expletives.)

▶ There are twenty-eight days in February.

▶ Reckless driving and speeding was the explanation for the traffic ticket.

SENTENCES WITH SUBJECT COMPLEMENTS A subject complement is a word or group of words that substitutes for the subject. A subject complement can easily be mistaken for the subject since it renames the subject.

▶ The *main requirement* of the job *is* a commitment to music and a demonstration of that commitment through station programming.

The verb "is" agrees with the singular subject "main requirement," not with the subject complement "commitment to music and a demonstration of that commitment through station programming."

VERBS AFTER *THAT, WHICH,* AND *WHO* The relative pronouns *that, which,* and *who* can be either singular or plural, depending on their **antecedents**—the word or words to which they refer.

▶ Students are one of the groups [plural] who are suffering from reductions in federal programs.

▶ A student [singular] who is ill should go to the health center.

It is not always immediately obvious if the antecedent is singular or plural. In the following example, "one of the" creates a plural meaning.

▶ The quality of the olive oil is *one of the* things [plural] that make some Italian dishes better than others.

Hint: To figure out what the verb should be, isolate the one word that can substitute for the subject—in this case "things"—and mentally state the simplified sentence that results: "Things make dishes better."

SINGULAR NOUNS ENDING IN -*S* Words that end in -*s* such as *academics, statistics, mathematics,* and *physics* are frequently singular.

▶ At some schools, *athletics is* stressed more than studying.

▶ *Statistics is* feared by many a graduate student.

A title containing plural nouns is singular.

▶ *Hard Times* is widely read by English majors.

Use the plural form when suggesting separate activities or characteristics.

▶ The statistics of war are shocking.

21b Irregular Verbs

Verbs change form to show changes in tense or time. Regular verbs form their past tense and past participle by adding -*d* (for example, *care, cared*), -*ed* (for example, *walk, walked*), or -*t* (for example, *burn, burnt*). Irregular verbs form their past tense and past participle in many different ways. Irregular verb forms must be memorized. The following table gives the past tense and past participle of some common irregular verbs.

Common Irregular Verbs

PRESENT TENSE	PAST TENSE	PAST PARTICIPLE
arise	arose	arisen
awake	awoke, awaked	awaked, awoke
be	was, were	been
beat	beat	beaten, beat
become	became	become
begin	began	begun
bend	bent	bent
bite	bit	bitten, bit
blow	blew	blown
break	broke	broken
bring	brought	brought
build	built	built
burst	burst	burst
buy	bought	bought
catch	caught	caught
choose	chose	chosen
cling	clung	clung
come	came	come
cost	cost	cost
deal	dealt	dealt
dig	dug	dug
dive	dived, dove	dived
do	did	done
drag	dragged	dragged
draw	drew	drawn
dream	dreamed, dreamt	dreamed, dreamt
drink	drank	drunk

PRESENT TENSE	PAST TENSE	PAST PARTICIPLE
drive	drove	driven
eat	ate	eaten
fall	fell	fallen
feel	felt	felt
fight	fought	fought
find	found	found
fly	flew	flown
forget	forgot	forgotten, forgot
freeze	froze	frozen
get	got	gotten, got
give	gave	given
go	went	gone
grow	grew	grown
hang (suspend)	hung	hung
hang (execute)	hanged	hanged
have	had	had
hear	heard	heard
hide	hid	hidden
hold	held	held
hurt	hurt	hurt
keep	kept	kept
know	knew	known
lay (put)	laid	laid
lead	led	led
lend	lent	lent
let (allow)	let	let
lie (recline)	lay	lain
lose	lost	lost
make	made	made
prove	proved	proved, proven
read	read	read
ride	road	ridden
ring	rang	rung
rise	rose	risen
run	ran	run
say	said	said
see	saw	seen
send	sent	sent
set (put)	set	set
shake	shook	shaken
shine	shone	shone
shoot	shot	shot

PRESENT TENSE	PAST TENSE	PAST PARTICIPLE
shrink	shrank	shrunk, shrunken
sing	sang	sung
sink	sank	sunk
sit (be seated)	sat	sat
slay	slew	slain
sleep	slept	slept
speak	spoke	spoken
spin	spun	spun
spring	sprang	sprung
stand	stood	stood
steal	stole	stolen
sting	stung	stung
strike	struck	struck, stricken
swear	swore	sworn
swim	swam	swum
swing	swung	swung
take	took	taken
teach	taught	taught
throw	threw	thrown
wake	woke, waked	waked, woken
wear	wore	worn
wring	wrung	wrung
write	wrote	written

22 Pronoun Agreement

Pronouns—*she, he, it, them,* and so forth—are words that substitute for nouns. Pronouns must agree with their **antecedents**—the word or words to which they refer—and with the
verb in the sentence by agreeing in number and case.

22a Pronoun-Antecedent Agreement

Use singular pronouns to refer to singular nouns and plural
pronouns to refer to plural nouns.

▶ *Steve* argued for *his* position, but his *friends* preferred *their* own
plans.

▶ *Everyone* voted for *his or her* favorite candidate.

"Everyone" is singular; therefore, "his" or "her" (singular pronouns) are used.

Singular and Plural Forms of Pronouns

SINGULAR			
SECOND PERSON	I	me	my	mine
SECOND PERSON	you	you	your	yours
THIRD PERSON	he/she/it	him/her/it	his/her/its	his/her/its
PLURAL			
FIRST PERSON	we	us	our	ours
SECOND PERSON	you	you	your	yours
THIRD PERSON	they	them	their	theirs

22b With the Conjunctions *And*, *Or*, and *Nor*

Use a plural pronoun to refer to two nouns or pronouns joined by *and*.

▶ *The instructor and the student* agreed that *they* should meet.

▶ *He and I* asked if *we* could collaborate on the next assignment.

Use a singular pronoun to refer to two singular nouns joined by *or* or *nor*.

▶ Either *Michael or Jason* can take *his* turn first.

If you have one singular and one plural noun joined by *or* or *nor*, place the plural noun in the second position and use a plural pronoun.

▶ Neither *Maggie nor her three sisters* have received *their* checks.

22c Indefinite Pronoun Antecedents

Indefinite pronouns that are singular should be referred to by singular pronouns.

▶ *Each* of the colleges has *its* own admissions policy.

Some indefinite pronouns are plural (*both*, *few*, *many*) and require plural pronouns.

▶ A *few* of the players have yet to pass *their* physicals.

Some indefinite pronouns may be either singular or plural (*all, any, some*). A pronoun referring to one of these indefinite pronouns is singular if the indefinite pronoun referred to stresses the action of an entire group as a whole; it is plural if it refers to the various situations of members of the group.

▶ *Some* of the *play* was entertaining.

▶ *Some* of the *costumes* are grotesque.

22d With Collective Nouns

Treat collective nouns (*class, team, audience, committee,* and so forth) as singular if you are stressing the group's acting as a unit; treat them as plural if you are stressing the actions of the group's individual members.

▶ The *class* will take *its* final exam on Monday.

▶ The *class* immediately began to register *their* protests.

Do not treat the same noun as both singular and plural in the same sentence.

▶ The class was stunned but then registered their protests.

REVISED   The students in the class were stunned but then registered their protests.

22e Gender-Inclusive Pronouns

When referring to a singular noun that may be either male or female, use *his or her*, not *his* alone. If you wish to avoid using *his or her* (which, when overused, can sound awkward), switch to the plural.

▶ A *doctor's* responsibility is to *his or her* patients.

REVISED   *Doctors* are responsible for *their* patients.

▶ A *parent* should take good care of *his* children.

REVISED   *Parents* should take good care of *their* children.

23 Pronoun Case

Case refers to the way a pronoun functions in a sentence—as a subject (**nominative case**), as an object (**objective case**), or to how possession (possessive case). Pronouns must be used in the proper case form.

► It is *she* who must be obeyed.

In this sentence, "she" functions as a subject and must be in the nominative case.

► We elected *her* president.

In this sentence, "her" is the object and thus is in the objective case.

► The president wanted to know if *his* changes to the agenda had been added.

In this sentence, "his" shows possession.

		CHECKLIST 20
Case Forms of Personal Pronouns		
NOMINATIVE CASE	**OBJECTIVE CASE**	**POSSESSIVE CASE**
I	me	my
we	us	our
you	you	your
he/she/it	him/her/it	his/her/its
they	them	their

23a With Appositives

Appositives mean the same thing as the word to which they refer.

► Dr. Jefferson, *my physics professor*, just retired.

Appositives and the nouns to which they refer (their antecedents) should be in the same case.

► The handout was for the only two sophomores in the class, Ramon and *me*.

Hint: When you read the sentence to yourself, test it with only a pronoun in the appositive position. Listen to the sound of your sentence. You would not say: "The handout was for I." You would say: "The handout was for me."

Use the subjective case when the pronoun acts as a subject.

▶ Loyal friends, Jennifer and *I* decided to stay in spite of the rain.

Hint: "I decided to stay."

Use the objective case when the pronoun acts as an object.

▶ The lawyer asked the witnesses, Addy and *me*, to testify.

Hint: "The lawyer asked me to testify."

(See Checklist 19, page 139, for a review of how to form plural pronouns in different cases.)

23b With Incomplete Comparisons

When using pronouns to compare two nouns, avoid using incomplete sentence structures or elliptical constructions. Such sentences omit words and require careful use of pronouns. Be sure sentences convey the meaning that you intend them to convey.

▶ James likes sailing more than *I.*

This sentence means that James likes sailing more than I like sailing. The writer has omitted "more than I like sailing."

▶ James likes sailing more than *me.*

This sentence means that James likes sailing more than he likes me. The writer has omitted "more than he likes me."

23c With Subjects of Infinitives

Subjects of infinitives should be in the objective case.

▶ We wanted *him* to see the photographs.

"Him" is the subject of the infinitive phrase "him to see the photographs." *Hint:* First identify the subject and the verb: "We wanted." Next identify the object by asking, Who or what did we want? The answer: "him to see the photographs." The entire phrase is the object of the sentence. The object happens to include its own subject—"him."

23d Before Gerunds

Pronouns before **gerunds** (*-ing* words used as nouns) must be in the possessive case.

▶ *His* walking away showed good judgment.

The "walking away" is owned by him. To show ownership, use the possessive case.

Sometimes an -*ing* word preceded by a pronoun is not a gerund phrase, but a participial phrase. Consider the following sentence:

▶ I saw *him* walking away.

In this sentence, the object is "him," which is modified by "walking away," a participial phrase.

23e Pronoun Reference

Pronoun reference in a sentence must be clear. Readers should have no trouble figuring out to whom or to what a pronoun refers. Revise sentences with ambiguous references, even if you have to repeat a reference rather than use the pronoun.

AMBIGUOUS	Americans admire movie stars because *they* are wealthy and attractive.
REVISED	Americans admire movie stars because *movie stars* are wealthy and attractive.

In the first sentence, "they" can refer to either "Americans" or "movie stars."

AMBIGUOUS	The new prison has updated facilities, but *they* still treat inmates harshly.
REVISED	The new prison has updated facilities, but *the prison officials* still treat inmates harshly.

Grammatically, "they" refers to "facilities" in the first sentence. Actually, "they" refers to "the prison officials," which is implied but not mentioned in that sentence.

PRONOUN REFERENCE WITH RELATIVE PRONOUNS *That*, *which*, *who*, *whoever*, *whom*, *whomever*, and *whose* are relative pronouns, pronouns that relate or connect parts of sentences. Use *who* or *whom* to refer to people; use *that* to refer to objects. Informally, *that* is sometimes used to refer to a class of people.

▶ I surprised *whoever* was there.

"Whoever" is the subject of the clause "was there."

▶ She was the only one in the class *who* had been to Mexico.

▶ The place *that* she wanted to see was Mexico.

Note: Use *who* or *whoever* in the subject position of a sentence; use *whom* or *whomever* if the pronoun functions as an object. When you want to refer to one or more things rather than to people, use *which* or *that.*

▶ The antiques *that* we bought in Philadelphia are from the eighteenth century.

The clause "that we bought in Philadelphia" is an essential clause (see the next section) and should not be set off with commas.

▶ Our antiques, *which* are primarily in the upstairs rooms, do not match the style of our contemporary home.

The clause "which are primarily in the upstairs rooms" is a nonessential clause (see the next section) and must be set off with commas.

PRONOUN REFERENCE WITH *THAT* AND *WHICH* IN ESSENTIAL AND NONESSENTIAL CLAUSES   Use *that* to introduce expressions that are essential to the meaning of a sentence. Use *which* to introduce nonessential expressions. Set off nonessential clauses with commas. (See section 27d, pages 156–57.)

▶ The game *that* I remember best was the only one we lost.

In this sentence, the writer wants to make a point that of all the games he or she remembers, there is one that stands out.

▶ The game, *which* I remember well, was the only one we lost.

In this sentence, the *which* expression is presented as an afterthought, something not essential to the meaning of the sentence. The commas set the idea aside, much as parentheses do.

Avoid using *that* or *which* to refer to a general state of affairs implied, but not necessarily specified, in your writing.

▶ I was concerned ~~that~~ because you had not called.

▶ ~~That~~ This sentence needs to be revised.

24 Adjectives and Adverbs

24a Adjectives

Adjectives modify nouns and pronouns. They can be words, phrases, or clauses.

▶ We had *rainy* weather.

▶ The *stone* walls have been standing for *more than two hundred* years.

The italicized words and phrases in the above sentences are adjectives.

Adjectives usually follow verb forms of *be*, *seem*, *appear*, and *become*; sensory words such as *taste*, *touch*, and *feel*; and a few other verbs, including *grow*, *prove*, *get*, *keep*, *remain*, and *turn*.

▶ I am *happy*.

▶ It tastes *good*.

▶ She has been proved *wrong*.

24b Adverbs

Adverbs modify verbs, adjectives, and other adverbs. Adverbs can be a single word, a phrase, or a clause. Adverbs are often formed by adding *-ly* to adjectives.

▶ It rained *softly*.

▶ It rained *in the evening*.

▶ *When it rained*, we went inside.

Sometimes the same word can function as either an adverb or an adjective, depending on its meaning in a sentence.

▶ Kristen is feeling *well*.

"Well" (meaning "healthy") is an adjective, modifying the subject.

▶ She did *well* on the test.

"Well" is an adverb, modifying the verb.

▶ Drive *slowly* in a school zone.

"Slowly" is an adverb, modifying the verb drive.

▶ The car functions best at *slow* speeds.

"Slow" is an adjective, modifying the noun "speeds."

24c Comparatives and Superlatives

Adverbs and adjectives have three forms: the **positive form** (which is the adverb or adjective itself), the **comparative** form (which compares two things), and the **superlative form** (which compares three or more things). In general, form the comparative or the superlative by adding *-er* and *-est* to the base.

▶ I ride *faster* than Jordan.

▶ Jeremy rides the *fastest*.

With words ending in *-ly*, however, the comparative and superlative are formed by adding the words *more* and *most* (or *less* and *least*) before the adverb.

▶ She rides *more quickly*.

POSITIVE	COMPARATIVE	SUPERLATIVE
fast	faster	fastest
quickly	more quickly	most quickly

With longer adjectives, the comparative and superlative are also formed by adding *more* and *most* (or *less* and *least*) before the adjective.

▶ the *most beautiful* view.

POSITIVE	COMPARATIVE	SUPERLATIVE
pretty	prettier	prettiest
beautiful	more beautiful	most beautiful

25 Grammar Tips for Speakers of English as a Second Language

Some features of English pose difficulties for students who learned another language before learning English. This section reviews some problem areas for English as a Second Language (ESL) students.

25a Articles (*a*, *an*, *the*)

Articles—*a*, *an*, *the*—indicate that the word following them is a noun. Learn how to use *a*, *an*, and *the* correctly with both countable and uncountable nouns. Also learn when no article is needed.

WHEN TO USE A, AN

1. Use *a* or *an* when a singular, countable noun is not known to the reader or listener.

   ▶ *A* cat is on the doorstep.

"A cat" is correct if you do not know the animal. "Cat" is a "countable" noun. You can count the number of cats in a kennel.

▶ *A* ticket costs fifty dollars.

"A ticket" is correct because you have not yet purchased the specific ticket you will use. "Ticket" is a countable noun. You can count the number of tickets available for sale.

2. Use *a* before countable nouns that begin with a consonant.

▶ *a* cat, *a* radio, *a* college campus

3. Use *an* before countable nouns that begin with a vowel and before consonants that begin with a silent *h*.

▶ *an* elephant, *an* hour

WHEN TO USE *THE*

1. Use *the* when the noun (singular or plural) is already familiar to the reader or listener.

▶ *The* cat is on *the* couch again.

▶ *The* ticket for tonight's show is on *the* table.

2. Use *the* with singular, uncountable nouns.

▶ *The* milk is in the refrigerator.

▶ *The* food is on the table.

WHEN NOT TO USE AN ARTICLE

1. Do not use an article with singular proper nouns that refer to a specific place.

▶ I visited Atlanta, Georgia, last summer.

Note: Use *the* with some geographical areas—for example, *the South, the Northeast, the United States.*

2. Do not use an article when you want to indicate a general category.

▶ ~~The car~~ Car emissions can pollute the environment.

Note: The original sentence indicates that a specific type of car emission can pollute the environment.

25b Adjectives and Adverbs

PLACEMENT OF ADJECTIVES AND ADVERBS IN SENTENCE
Adjectives are placed differently in English than in some other
languages. In English, the standard order is adverb-adjective-
noun, as in *especially healthy students.*

Adverbs can appear in the following positions:

● At the beginning of a sentence

   ▶ *Cautiously*, she moved up the steps.

● At the end of a sentence

   ▶ She moved up the steps *cautiously.*

● Before the main verb

   ▶ She *cautiously* moved up the steps.

● After the main verb

   ▶ She moved *cautiously* up the steps.

● Before, between, and after helping and main verbs

   ▶ *Cautiously*, she would move up the steps.

   ▶ She would move *cautiously* up the steps.

   ▶ She would *cautiously* move up the steps.

Note: Not all adverbs can be placed after helping verbs.

   ▶ The student can ~~find~~ usually ^{find} errors in his sentences.

ADJECTIVES USED WITH COUNT AND NONCOUNT NOUNS Notice whether the noun you are using is a "count" noun (such
as *bananas, steak, peas*) or a "noncount" noun (such as *fruit,
meat, vegetables*). Then determine which adjective is appropriate to use with the noun in question.

Many/much Use *many* with count nouns; use *much* with noncount nouns.

   ▶ There are *many bananas* on the table. [You can count
bananas.]

   ▶ There is too *much fruit* on the table. [You can't count fruit; it's a
general category.]

   ▶ There are *many people* in the class. [You can count the
people.]

   ▶ There is *much human error* involved. [You can't count human
error; it's a quality.]

▶ There are *many days* when we have good weather in April. [Days can be counted.]

▶ There is not *much good weather* in January. [You can't count weather; it's a general concept.]

few/a little Use *a few* with count nouns; use *a little* with noncount nouns.

▶ You can give me *a few ideas*. [You can count ideas.]

▶ Can you give me *a little help*. [You can't count help; it's a concept.]

Number/amount Use *number* with count nouns; use *amount* with noncount nouns.

▶ You have a large *number of students* at your university.

▶ It takes a large *amount of money* to go to college.

25c Verbs

Verb forms in English can cause problems for students for whom English is a second language. Below are the major areas to focus on if you have problems with verbs.

HELPING VERBS Helping or auxiliary verbs combine with verb forms to form different tenses and include *am, are, be, been, being, can, could, did, do, does, had, has, have, is, may, might, must, shall, should, was, were, will,* and *would*.

A helping verb must come before the base form or the infinitive form of the verb. For more on verb tense, see below.

▶ She *has* helped me for many years.

"Has" comes before the base form of the verb *help*.

▶ They *must* learn how to study.

"Must" comes before the main verb "learn."

▶ I *have* to go home.

"Have" comes before the infinitive "to go."

Do is used as a helping verb to form questions and negative statements.

▶ *Did* you enjoy your trip to Mexico?

▶ My sister *did not* travel with me to Mexico.

After *do* and some helping verbs (such as *can, could, may, or might*), a verb is often used alone, without sentence modifier following it. Note that in the following examples there is no *-s* added to the verbs "care" or "happen."

▶ She does *care*.

▶ It could *happen*.

CHANGES IN VERB TENSE Rather than trying to memorize rules for using different tenses, listen to and practice correct combinations. Below is a table for reference.

PRESENT	PAST	FUTURE
SIMPLE:		
I study	I studied	I will study
PROGRESSIVE *(refers to an action in progress or unfinished):*		
I am studying	I was studying	I will be studying
PERFECT *(refers to an action that began in the past but continues in the present):*		
I have studied	I had studied	I will have studied
PERFECT PROGRESSIVE *(refers to an action that began in the past, continues in the present, and may continue in the future):*		
I have been studying	I had been studying	I will have been studying

25d Idiomatic Expressions

IDIOMATIC PHRASES All languages have expressions that are understandable to native speakers but almost untranslatable to others. These expressions are referred to as idioms or idiomatic phrases. If you are an ESL student, try to listen for these phrases and memorize them. Gradually, you will use them in the proper situations, just as people who have spoken English for their entire lives do. Often these idioms are metaphors—imaginative uses of language—such as *keep your eye on the ball* (meaning "be observant") or *cut the mustard* (meaning "do the job"). Other times they are merely phrases, such as *think it over, get going, on the contrary*, and *above all*.

Many verbs in English are commonly used with a preposition and are, in effect, a special kind of idiom. Two-word combinations, such as *graduate from, insist on, back off, turn on*, and *turn off* are not easy for speakers for whom English is not their first language. The best advice is to keep a list of two-word verbs and their meanings and to memorize them.

25e Complete Sentences

In some languages, one word can serve as both subject and predicate. In English, only imperative sentences can omit the subject (the subject, "you," is understood). Other sentences require both a subject and a verb.

► *Look* at the stop sign.
► ~~Bought~~ a ticket. *I bought*
► The animals outside in the cold. *were*

When the subject follows the verb, an expletive (*there is, there are, it is,* and so forth) is usually required.

► *It is* usually cold in Minnesota.

Introductory words can sometimes confuse nonnative speakers into omitting expletives.

► Although we were comfortable, was always cold in Minnesota. *it*

Do not omit the verb in sentences like

► He a very good cook. *is*

Punctuation

26 End Punctuation

Every sentence must end with either a period, a question mark, or an exclamation point.

26a The Period [.]

Use a period at the end of statements, mild commands, or indirect questions.

- ▶ The banks are closed today.

- ▶ Please shut down your computer at the end of the day.

- ▶ I wonder what happened to him.

26b The Question Mark [?]

Use a question mark at the end of direct questions and within parentheses and dashes to indicate uncertainty within a sentence.

- ▶ What happened to him?

- ▶ It was early (before 6 A.M.?).

26c The Exclamation Point [!]

Use an exclamation point at the end of assertions of surprise or other strong emotions.

- ▶ "He's alive!" Dr. Frankenstein screamed.

- ▶ Don't touch that disk! The disk drive is spinning.

Do not overuse exclamation points. Reserve them for special effects, such as in the above examples, and remember that one exclamation point works better than a string of three or four to signal heightened feeling.

27 The Comma [,]

Writers use commas according to a handful of basic rules involving signaling pauses within sentences and clarifying structure.

27a With Coordinating Conjunctions in Compound Sentences

Unless the sentences are short, use a comma between two independent clauses joined by a coordinating conjunction (*and, but, for, nor, or, so, yet*) to signal the end of one clause and the beginning of the next.

▶ The judge listened attentively, but many of the jurors had trouble following the testimony.

The comma can be omitted in short, parallel sentences.

▶ The judge listened attentively but many of the jurors did not.

A comma is *not* used when a coordinating conjunction links the parts of a compound verb.

▶ The judge listened attentively/ but ruled against the motion.

27b After Most Introductory Material

Use a comma after introductory material to signal to the reader that the main part of the sentence is beginning. The comma may be omitted if the introductory material is brief and flows directly into the main clause.

▶ Nevertheless, we decided to continue.

▶ Although most film critics disliked the movie, it enjoyed great success at the box office.

▶ In some cities the movie enjoyed great success at the box office.

27c Between Items in a Series

A comma is used to separate each item in a series. Usually, *and* or *or* is used before the last item.

▶ I am studying statistics, astronomy, and physics.

▶ Next term, I plan to take algebra, chemistry, or geology.

Each item in a series can itself consist of many words.

> ▶ The mayor was delighted that the city council approved the new
> parking garage, defeated changes in the zoning ordinance, and
> delayed consideration of increases in sewerage rates.

When each item in a series includes commas, a semicolon is
used to separate the items.

> ▶ The mayor was delighted that the city council approved the new
> parking garage, the one to be built near city hall; defeated
> changes in the zoning ordinance, changes that would have
> helped save many old neighborhoods; and delayed
> consideration of increases in sewerage rates.

A series may consist of only two words, as in the case of co
ordinate (or reversible) adjectives before a noun.

> ▶ *Halloween* is a suspenseful, terrifying movie.
>
> *or*
>
> ▶ *Halloween* is a terrifying, suspenseful movie.

Do not use a comma with adjectives whose order in a se
quence is not reversible.

> ▶ We saw a new Australian movie.

The adjectives "new" and "Australian" are not reversible. You
would not say "an Australian new movie."

27d Before and After Nonessential Words and Phrases

Use a pair of commas to indicate that the words between the
commas are nonessential and could be omitted without loss of
meaning. Nonessential material may be informative or inter
esting, but it is always extra information, not information that
narrows and, thus, helps to identify the subject under consid
eration.

Remember two things when using commas to distinguish be
tween essential and nonessential material: (1) always use a pair
of commas to separate nonessential material, one on each side
of the material, and (2) when in doubt about whether some
thing is nonessential or not, leave the commas out. (See also
section 23e, page 144.)

> ▶ Graduates *who are adept at using computers* have an
> advantage in the job market.

The example above assumes that these graduates have an advantage over those graduates who are not adept at using computers.

▶ Graduates, *who are adept at using computers*, have an
advantage in the job market.

That is, graduates generally have this particular advantage over nongraduates. The information about their computer skills is offered here as something extra; the sentence can be read without the words between the commas.

27e Other Comma Rules

Some comma rules do not fit into categories. Think of these rules as ones that apply only in certain circumstances.

1. Use commas to prevent misreading.

   ▶ Soon after, Stephen Bill left the room.

2. Use commas to indicate omitted words.

   ▶ Tim donated $50; Robert, $100.

3. Use commas to set off the year when the month and
   day are also given.

   ▶ The hearing was set for May 12, 1998, but it actually
   began in July.

4. Use commas to set off the name of a state, county, or
   country that follows the name of a city.

   ▶ Our Fresno, California, location has three stores to serve
   you.

5. Use commas with contrasting expressions (*but, not,
   rather than*) that emphasize a sense of contrast.

   ▶ The managers promoted Jonah, rather than Mike.

27f Comma Problems

1. Do not be fooled by the pause and punctuate the subject
   of a sentence as an introductory phrase.

   ▶ To create a successful Web site⁄requires considerable
   planning.

2. Do not use a comma between compound verbs (verbs joined by *or* or *and*).

   ▶ We studied for the test/and developed our confidence.

   In this sentence, "studied" and "developed" are compound verbs and are, therefore, not separated by a comma.

3. Do not use commas inconsistently.

   ▶ Since it is a beautiful day ∧ I think I'll go for a walk.

   ▶ Because I have little time ∧ I rarely exercise during the work week.

   If you use a comma after an introductory phrase, do so consistently throughout your paper.

4. Although commas should be used to separate the non-essential material from the rest of the sentence, do not use a comma to separate two complete sentences. Doing so creates a comma splice. (See section 18b, page 116.)

   ▶ Talk is cheap<del>,</del> . Action ∧ <del>action</del> is what counts.

   ▶ You shouldn't be concerned about grammar as you draft<del>,</del> . You ∧ <del>you</del> should focus on content and organization.

5. Do not forget the second comma in nonessential phrases. Think of these two commas as if they were parentheses.

   ▶ Computer viruses, often compared to physical diseases ∧ are common on our campus.

CHECKLIST 21 **Quick Review of Comma Rules**

USE A COMMA
● between two independent clauses joined by one of the seven coordinating conjunctions: *and, but, for, nor, or, so, yet*.
● after most introductory material.
● between coordinate items in a series.
● before and after nonessential words and phrases.
● as called for according to convention or to prevent misreading.

28 The Semicolon [;] and Colon [:]

28a The Semicolon [;]

In addition to using the semicolon between series items with internal commas (see page 156), the semicolon can be used to join closely connected independent clauses that are not otherwise connected by a coordinating conjunction. The basic rule in using semicolons is to be sure that you have complete sentences (independent clauses) on both sides of the semicolon.

▶ The rain never ceased; it continued throughout the night and into the next week.

▶ Time went quickly; before she knew it, she was too old to find a good job.

The semicolon strengthens the connection between the two ideas that, if joined by a period, might be read as two separate, less related sentences. Be careful, however, not to use a comma, which in such cases would create a comma splice. (See section 8b, page 116.)

Hence, however, indeed, moreover, still, therefore, thus, and similar terms are adverbs (sometimes called conjunctive adverbs) that belong entirely to the second sentence. Therefore, they cannot be used like a coordinating conjunction to join two sentences. When used after a semicolon, they are followed by a comma. When used as interrupters within independent clauses, they are set off with commas.

▶ Homer found it difficult to beg forgiveness; however, Marj eventually forgave him.

▶ Homer found it difficult to beg forgiveness; Marj, however, eventually forgave him.

28b Semicolon Problems

Do not use a semicolon in sentences that do not contain two independent clauses. Use a comma instead.

▶ The interview went well;/better than I expected.

The phrase "better than I expected" is not an independent clause. It is a phrase that modifies the entire sentence and that can be separated from the sentence with a comma.

► As time passed‚⁄I knew I was going to like her.

The first part of the above sentence is an introductory clause (acting as an adverb) and must be connected to the independent clause with a comma.

28c The Colon [:]

Within a sentence, a colon announces a list, a question, or a complete sentence that follows it.

1. Use a colon after an independent clause to introduce a list, a direct quotation, or an explanation.

   ► These are the key factors to consider when purchasing software: price, performance, and support.

   ► Confucius says: "It is easy to be rich and not haughty; it is difficult to be poor and not grumble."

   ► When the time is right, you'll know it: You'll be ready to get married, and you'll want to do it without delay.

   It is appropriate to capitalize the first word of a complete sentence following a colon.

2. Use a colon after salutations in formal business letters.

   ► Dear Dr. Bartholemew:

   ► Dear Admissions Committee:

   Instead of saying "Dear Sir or Madam," use a noun to substitute for the person to whom you are addressing the letter.

3. Use a colon to separate the title of a work from the subtitle.

   ► *A Writer's Tool: The Computer in Composition Instruction*

28d Colon Problems

1. Do not use a colon when a period or other punctuation is more appropriate.

   ► We bought enough paper to last for several years. Paper~~: paper~~ for laser printers is less expensive when you buy it in quantity.

In this case, the two sentences are not sufficiently linked to justify using a colon.

2. Do not use a colon to separate a verb from its objects or complements.

▶ Three factors to consider when purchasing software are:/ price, performance, and support.

or

▶ When purchasing software, consider these three factors: price, performance, and support.

29 The Apostrophe [']

The apostrophe has two different functions: it indicates possession (ownership), and it indicates omission of a letter or letters (in contractions). Mastering a few standard rules for apostrophe use can help you detect and diagnose many common errors.

29a Indicating Possession

● With singular nouns, add -*'s*.

▶ The woman's briefcase was stolen.

● With plural nouns ending in -*s*, add an apostrophe only.

▶ The two countries' flags fly side by side.

● With plural nouns not ending in -*s*, add -*'s*.

▶ The children's bikes are in the driveway.

● With compound nouns, add -*'s* to the last element.

▶ My brother-in-law's hammering went on until dusk.

● With compound nouns indicating joint ownership, add -*'s* to the last element.

▶ Don and Marie's portrait hangs above their fireplace mantle.

● If there are two or more separate owners, add -*'s* to each noun.

▶ Our son's and daughter's dating habits are baffling.

- When a singular or plural name ends in -s, add either -'s or an apostrophe only.

  ▶ Charles's book is on the desk.

  or

  ▶ Charles' book is on the desk.

  ▶ The Douglas's house is in the country.

  or

  ▶ The Douglas' house is in the country.

Note: Convention calls for *Zeus'*, *Moses'*, and *Jesus'* as well as a single apostrophe with names like *Euripides* that are difficult to pronounce with an added syllable.

29b Indicating Omission

In contractions.

  ▶ We're going home because I've got a cold.

Informally, in dates.

  ▶ The winter of '98 was surprisingly mild.

In standard or invented abbreviations.

  ▶ The story began on the front page, but the editor continued it on a later page, indicating the specific place with the words "cont'd, p. 3."

29c Other Uses of the Apostrophe

Use -'s to form the plural of lowercase letters, abbreviations containing periods, and words used as examples of words.

  ▶ add *x*'s

  ▶ compare I.D.'s

  ▶ too many *no*'s

Note: It is becoming acceptable to use -s only to form the plural of numbers and capital letters.

  ▶ 1960s

  ▶ the three Rs

Quick Review of Possessive Apostrophe Rules

SINGULAR

- Add *-'s* to singular nouns not ending in *-s*.

  ▶ the dog's collar

- Add *-'s* or a single apostrophe to singular nouns ending in *-s*.

  ▶ my friend Bess's [or Bess'] mother

PLURAL

- Add a single apostrophe to plural nouns ending in *-s*.

  ▶ the boys' clubhouse

- Add a single apostrophe or *-'s* to names.

  ▶ the Santos' house

  ▶ the Santos's house

- Add *-'s* to plural nouns not ending in *-s*.

  ▶ our children's friends

COMPOUND NOUNS

- In general, add *-'s* to the last element.

  ▶ my son-in-law's wife

- Add *-'s* to the last element to show joint possession.

  ▶ Abbott and Costello's comedy routines

- Add *-'s* to each element if there are two or more owners.

  ▶ Roberta's and Carol's tastes were very different.

29d Common Errors with Apostrophes

Many people confuse the possessive form *its* ("belonging to it") with the contraction *it's* ("it is" or "it has"). Similarly, people sometimes confuse the possessive *your* ("belonging to you") with the contraction *you're* ("you are"). Whenever you use any of these forms, check your sentence to determine whether you have used the correct form. Read the sentence, substituting the full phrase (*you are, it has, it is*) for the contraction (*you're, it's*).

If the sentence does not make sense, then you know that you have to revise it.

▶ It's fur stood on end when the dog came into the room.

The sentence "It has fur stood on end" does not make sense.

Or you may have to substitute the contraction (or the uncontracted form of the word) for the possessive pronoun.

▶ Its been a long time since we met.

30 Quotation Marks [" "]

30a Quoting Exact Words

1. Use quotation marks to indicate someone's exact words, whether written, spoken, or thought.

   ▶ She said, "I'm happy that the course is almost over."

2. Use single quotation marks [' . . . '] to indicate a quotation within a quotation.

   ▶ She said, "I want you to remember that Frost's poem 'Out, Out' contains an allusion to Shakespeare's *Macbeth*."

3. Use indention, instead of quotation marks, for quoting more than four typed lines of continuous prose or more than three printed lines. Shorter passages of poetry can also be indented for emphasis.

   ▶ The best part of her talk related to the uses of the Internet for E-mail:

   > If students are going to benefit from their access to e-mail, then they have to learn how to do more than send and receive mail. They need to learn how to subscribe to lists, how to print text from screen, and how to create groups of students to whom they can mail their text. (Hawisher 386)

30b Formal Definitions

Use quotation marks to indicate formal definitions or words not to be taken at face value.

▶ *Intrepid* means "bold" or "fearless."

▶ Then this "genius" forgot the keys.

Punctuating Direct Quotations

● When a direct quotation is followed by a "tag" (*he said*, *she said*, and so forth), place the punctuation inside the quotation marks.

 ▶ "Let's take a closer look," she said.

● When a direct quotation is interrupted by a tag, set off the tag with a pair of commas, inserting the first comma before the first close quotation mark.

 ▶ "May I," she asked, "take a closer look?"

● With a somewhat lengthy quotation, use a colon rather than a comma to introduce it.

 ▶ There are, according to Joseph Weizenbaum, severe limits on what we should ask of computers: "Since we do not have any ways of making computers wise, we ought not now to give computers tasks that demand wisdom."

● Semicolons are placed *outside* close quotation marks.

 ▶ You said, "The check is in the mail"; I can only respond, "Not in my mail."

● Colons are placed *outside* close quotation marks.

 ▶ According to Ann, these are John's "four basic food groups": burgers, pizza, fried chicken, and beer.

● Periods and commas are placed *inside* quotation marks.

 ▶ The speech ended with the words "I rest my case."

● When the quoted sentence ends in a question mark or an exclamation point, no comma is used.

 ▶ "May I take a closer look?" she asked.

● When the entire sentence is a question, a question mark is placed *outside* close quotation marks.

 ▶ What does the last line mean: "And miles to go before I sleep"?

● Quotations longer than four typed lines should be set off from the rest of your essay without quotation marks (unless they occur *within* the passage). Indent the quoted passage an additional half inch or five spaces on the left side only (total indention: ten spaces).

30c Titles

Use quotation marks for titles of short works that are not part of a collection, individual items (stories, short poems, articles, songs, essays, and so forth) that usually appear in collections, episodes of radio and television shows, and subdivisions of a book.

▶ "A Rose for Emily" is a famous story by William Faulkner.

▶ "Why I Want a Wife" is an essay by Judy Syfers.

▶ My favorite *X-Files* episode is "The Paper Clip."

▶ The chapter "The Creation of Sentences" was very helpful.

30d Quotations Within Sentences

Except for quotation marks, quotations integrated into sentences do not require additional punctuation.

▶ He knows that someday "things will even out."

Do not use quotation marks in describing what other people said (indirect discourse).

▶ His only reply was that someday he would get even.

31 Other Punctuation Marks

31a The Dash [—]

Some software programs allow you to create the solid dash used in printed materials—called an **em-dash**. Otherwise, create a dash by typing two hyphens, one after the other, with no space before or after them.

The dash is used to emphasize a shift in tone or thought or to announce a list, a restatement, or an amplification—all matters that could be handled with other punctuation marks but with a slightly different effect. If used judiciously, dashes can help writers control the way their words are received by readers. Use a dash to get a reader's attention. A pair of dashes can be used in the middle of a sentence to emphasize—by setting off—an insertion in the middle of the sentence. Dashes are less formal than commas, but used in pairs they can serve a similar purpose.

▶ At the conference sat Roosevelt, Churchill, and Stalin—the leaders of the war against Hitler.

▶ He had practiced hard for the recital—did anyone realize how hard?—yet he was still nervous.

31b Parentheses [( )]

Parentheses are used to separate (or set aside) words or phrases from the rest of a sentence. Readers assume that the words between the parentheses are supplementary, intended to comment on or clarify a point. Occasionally, entire sentences are placed in parentheses to signal to a reader that additional information is being provided.

Use parentheses sparingly; substitute paired commas in those cases in which you want an additional comment to be more closely linked to the main flow of the sentence.

▶ Our local newspaper (at least it purports to be a newspaper) uncovered corruption.

1. Use parentheses to define terms that a reader cannot be expected to know.

   ▶ Several epidemiologists (scientists who study epidemics) were called in to assess the danger of rabies in the city.

2. Use parentheses to note a point that you would like a reader to consider, even though it is not essential to the gist of your text.

   ▶ A knowledge of computer programming (no longer thought to be an essential component of computer literacy) can enhance a technical writer's credibility with engineers.

3. Use parentheses to enclose in-text citations.

   ▶ *What Will Be* (Dertouzos) provides an exciting picture of technological change.

31c Ellipsis Points [. . .]

Ellipsis points are three equally spaced dots used to indicate that something in a passage is missing, such as part of a writer's exact words in a quotation. Note that you need one space after each dot. For use of ellipsis points in research papers, see section 9d, page 48.

Use ellipsis points in a documented paper when you want to omit material from a long quotation. Use ellipsis points only in the middle of a quote and at the end. Take care not to distort the meaning of the original text through your use of ellipsis points: if the text says that "Movie X was technically flawed and not enjoyable," do not write, "Movie X was . . . enjoyable."

▶ I disagree with the argument that the "students of the twenty-first century . . . will rarely use pencil and paper."

Use of ellipsis points also indicates that something is unfinished; it is acceptable—if it is not overused—in informal writing. In the example below, the first period concludes the sentence (without a space); it is then followed by the three ellipsis points with a space between each.

▶ And that's the way things went for me. . . .

31d Square Brackets [ ]

Square brackets are used to enclose words that you, as editor, have inserted into a quote for the purpose of clarity or of producing a grammatically correct sentence.

▶ Then the speaker concluded: "Our efforts at such [campaign financing] reforms have never appeared more promising."

Brackets are also used around parenthetical material within parentheses.

▶ These nudes are clearly Rubenesque (after the Flemish painter Peter Paul Rubens [1577–1640]).

The Latin term *sic* ("thus") is traditionally used inside brackets to indicate an obvious error in the original source, although at times it is more helpful just to give the correction inside the brackets.

▶ The sign said: This sail [*sic*] ends tomorrow.

31e The Slash [/]

The slash is sometimes used to indicate alternative words of equal weight.

▶ Schools are offering more pass/fail courses.

▶ Each student has his/her own computer.

Do not use *his/her* or *he/she* constructions routinely, however, since they generally distract your readers. To avoid referring to the generic pronoun *he*, rewrite the above sentence, using the plural. (See section 22e, page 140.)

▶ All of the students have their own computers.

A slash is also used to indicate lines of poetry when they are not indented, but are run into the text. Be sure to put a space before and after the slash.

▶ I've often wondered what Robert Frost meant by repeating the last two lines of "Stopping by Woods on a Snowy Evening": "And miles to go before I sleep, / And miles to go before I sleep."

Mechanics

32 Capitalization

Academic writing tasks require correct use of capital letters. Use these guidelines, and consult a dictionary when you have questions.

32a The First Word in a Sentence

The first word in a sentence must be capitalized. If you quote a complete sentence, you must capitalize the first word in the quotation.

▶ According to Tosca Moon Lee, "Even wiring private homes with the fiber-optic cable that will be necessary for such a quick exchange of high amounts of information could cost $100 billion."

32b Proper Nouns and Modifiers Derived from Them

A proper noun is a noun that names a specific person, place, or thing. Capitalize all proper nouns.

▶ *President Siegel* asked students to work on flood-relief efforts.

▶ Parts of *Colorado* suffered flooding in 1997.

▶ *Canada* was settled by both the English and the French.

▶ The *Kennesaw State College Student Government Association* established a flood-relief committee.

Modifiers derived from proper nouns are usually capitalized.

▶ Delegates from twenty *African* countries met at the United Nations.

~~African~~" is a modifier created by adding *-n* to the proper noun.

▶ The *Canadian* parliament is modeled on parliament structures in place in Great Britain.

2c Titles of Works

~~C~~apitalize the first and last words in a title and all other words ~~ex~~cept conjunctions, articles, and prepositions of four letters or ~~le~~ss.

▶ *The Night Before Christmas*

▶ *Bonnie and Clyde*

▶ "Battle Hymn of the Republic"

2d Personal Titles

1. Titles used before personal names must be capitalized.

   ▶ My ~~orthodontist~~ optometrist is *Dr.* Ross.

   ▶ Former *President* Richard Nixon's record was tarnished by the Watergate incident.

   ▶ I'll always remember *Aunt* Maria.

   However, titles used after personal names are usually lowercase.

   ▶ Daniel Patrick Moynihan, the Democratic *senator* from New York

2. Titles that refer to a high position may be capitalized even when they are used without the name of the person holding that title.

   ▶ the Pope

   ▶ the President

   ▶ the Director

2e Other Capitalization Rules

THE FIRST WORD IN LINES OF POETRY Capitalize the first ~~w~~ord in each line of a poem, whether or not the poetic line

forms a complete sentence, unless the author has intentional
chosen not to capitalize the words.

▶ Whose woods these are I think I know

▶ anyone lived in a pretty how town

In the second example, "anyone" should not be capitalized b
cause E. E. Cummings, the author, did not capitalize this lin
the first line of his poem "anyone lived in a pretty how town

SPECIFIC SCHOOL OR COLLEGE COURSES Capitalize the sp
cific title of a course. Do not capitalize the names of courses
you are referring to them generally rather than specifically, e
cept for language courses.

▶ My *art* course is *Art 301*. My *French* course is *French 350*.

▶ I'm taking two *English* courses: *American Literature* and
Advanced Composition.

32f Capitalization Errors

Do not capitalize the following:

1. The words *a*, *an*, and *the* when used with proper nouns

   ▶ a Democrat

   ▶ the *New Yorker*

2. The seasons of the year

   ▶ the fall semester

3. Decades

   ▶ the twenties

**CHECKLIST
24**   **Quick Review of Capitalization Rules**

ALWAYS CAPITALIZE
● the first word in a sentence.
● all proper nouns.
● titles used before personal names.
● the specific title of a course.

USUALLY CAPITALIZE
● modifiers derived from proper nouns.
● the first word in a line of poetry.

33 Italics (Underlining), Abbreviations, Numbers

33a Italics for Titles of Full-Length Works

Italicize or underline titles of full-length works, including books, periodicals, films, TV or radio shows, works of visual art, plays, poems published separately as books, and so forth.

▶ *Third Rock from the Sun*

▶ the *Washington Post*

▶ Picasso's *Guernica*

Use quotation marks to note shorter works such as magazine or newspaper articles, short stories, episodes of TV shows, and so on.

▶ The *Third Rock from the Sun* episode "Brains and Eggs" is my favorite.

▶ The article "How to Help Your Child Learn to Read," published in the *Transcript*, is invaluable.

33b Other Rules for Italics

LETTERS OR WORDS REFERRED TO AS OBJECTS Italicize or underline letters or words used as letters or words.

▶ Remember to cross that *t* and to dot that *i*.

▶ It seems as if every other word she uses is either *like* or *you know*.

TERMS ABOUT TO BE FORMALLY DEFINED Italicize or underline terms if you are about to define them. Remember to put the definition in quotation marks.

▶ The verb *vex* means "to puzzle."

NAMES OF SHIPS AND VEHICLES Italicize or underline the names of ships and vehicles.

▶ Lindbergh's *Spirit of St. Louis* now hangs in the Smithsonian.

FOREIGN WORDS AND PHRASES Italicize or underline foreign words and phrases not yet considered part of English, and set off their translation (if given) with quotation marks.

▶ Visitors to Quebec should take time to review their French—in particular, traffic signs such as *Arrête* ("Stop").

CHECKLIST 25

Titles: Quotation Marks, Italics, Capitalization

● Enclose in quotation marks titles of short works that are not part of a collection, poems, short stories, articles, songs, essays, episodes of radio and television shows, and subdivisions of a book.

▶ "When Lilacs Last in the Dooryard Bloom'd" is a poem about the death of Abraham Lincoln.

● Italicize (underline) titles of large works such as books, periodicals, films, television or radio shows, works of visual art, plays, poems published separately as books.

▶ *Leaves of Grass* is probably Whitman's most widely circulated collection of poetry.

● Capitalize the first word, the last word, and all other words in a title *except* coordinating conjunctions, articles (*a, an, the*), and prepositions of four letters or less.

▶ *Death of a Salesman*

▶ *Two Years Before the Mast*

▶ *Faulkner: A Biography*

▶ *The Egg and I*

33c Abbreviations

Use abbreviations sparingly and only when you are sure your readers will understand what you are referring to. Increasingly, abbreviations are accepted as alternate forms of longer terms and, thus, they are written without spaces or periods between the letters. This practice is especially common when abbreviations are composed of all capital letters (such as acronyms), capital-letter abbreviations of technical terms (URL for Uniform Resource Locater), and names of agencies (FBI) and organizations (NATO).

To use a less widely known abbreviation throughout a paper, write out the full name for your first reference and immediately follow it with its abbreviation in parentheses.

▶ The Federal Trade Commission (FTC) was established in 1914.

APPROPRIATE ABBREVIATIONS

1. Titles used before and after names are appropriate and can be used freely.

   ▶ Mr., Ms., Rev., Jr., MBA

   Do not use titles when you are citing. Say, "As Kennedy says," not "As Dr. Kennedy says."

2. Common abbreviations of time and measurement are acceptable and can be used freely.

   ▶ B.C.E or BCE

   ▶ C.E or CE

   ▶ a.m. or A.M.

   ▶ 3 p.m. or 3 P.M.

   ▶ no. (when followed by a specific figure)

3. Use capital letters for common acronyms. Acronyms of three letters or more are customarily written without periods.

   ▶ IBM, YMCA, PBS

INAPPROPRIATE ABBREVIATIONS   Do not abbreviate the following:

1. Personal names
   ▶ ~~Steve~~ Stephen Jones led the investigation.

2. Days of the week, months of the year, and holidays
   ▶ Classes do not meet on ~~Dec.~~ December 25.

3. Names of academic subjects
   ▶ I am taking ~~econ, poly sci,~~ economics, political science, and English.

4. Names of most states and countries (*Washington, D.C.*, and the *USA* being exceptions) in an academic paper
   ▶ She lives in ~~PA~~ Pennsylvania during the summer.

5. Divisions of a written text (like chapter and page)
   ▶ The poem is cited in ~~chap. one~~ chapter 1 on ~~p.~~ page 3.

33d Numbers

IN GENERAL Spell out numbers of one or two words up to ninety-nine, unless there are several numbers within a sentence. For numbers requiring three or more words, use numerals.

▶ twenty

▶ 120

▶ fifty-five

▶ Enrollment figures show that we have 910 returning freshman, 100 transfer students, and 30 graduate students.

The numbers "100" and "30" are not spelled out because there are several numbers in this sentence.

AT THE BEGINNING OF SENTENCES If a sentence begins with a number, either spell out the number or, better, reword the sentence.

▶ ~~150~~ species of water lily are found in the pond.
  One hundred fifty
  ∧

or

▶ The pond is home to 150 species of water lily.

USED FOR CLARITY Use numbers, even in nontechnical writing, to specify exactness in such things as pages and divisions of texts (*page 12*), addresses (*1600 Pennsylvania Avenue*), dates (*May 22, 1978*), time (*9:45 a.m.*), and measurements (*95 percent*). In dealing with the many special cases, remember to be consistent within your own paper.

34 The Hyphen and Spelling

34a The Hyphen [-]

A hyphen is used to form compound adjectives or compound nouns and with words formed by adding a capital letter.

▶ in-laws, H-bomb

Use a hyphen to show that two or more words are being used as a single adjective before a noun. But when a compound adjective follows a noun, the hyphen is often not used.

▶ an IBM-compatible computer

▶ a computer that is IBM compatible

Use a hyphen to prevent misreading and awkward constructions.

▶ a little-used printer

▶ re-covered book

Use a hyphen with certain prefixes.

▶ self-sacrifice

▶ ex-president

▶ all-inclusive

Note that some compound words (like *real estate*) are written as two words, others (like *manic-depressive*) are hyphenated, while still others (like *fainthearted*) are one word. It is best to rely on a dictionary or spell checker.

Use a hyphen when writing out compound numbers and fractions.

▶ One-fourth of the class graduated with honors.

▶ Numbers from twenty-one to ninety-nine should be hyphenated.

If you choose to divide a word at the end of a line, be sure to hyphenate it between syllables. Check a dictionary whenever you are unsure of how to divide a word.

Do not hyphenate the last word of a line; transpose the entire word to the last line.

If part of a compound term falls at the end of the line, hyphenate between words, not between syllables.

Note: Word processing programs allow writers to include different types of hyphens. See pages 94–95 for a discussion.

34b Spelling Rules

Correct spelling is important on final drafts. Even if you are a good speller, be sure to run the spell checker before submitting your paper to either your peers or your teacher. Proofread your paper carefully, remembering to see if you have used words such as *their* and *there* correctly, for a spell checker cannot tell if you have used the wrong word. Finally, make frequent use of your dictionary.

Here are a few spelling pointers to keep in mind:

1. Use *i* before *e* except after *c* or when sounding like *ay* as in *neighbor* or *weigh*.

   ▶ believe, receive, sleigh

   EXCEPTIONS   either, seize, height, foreign, weird

2. Words that end in a silent *-e* usually drop the *-e* when a suffix is added if the suffix begins with a vowel. If the suffix begins with a consonant, however, retain the final *-e*.

   ▶ believe, believable; achieve, achievement

   EXCEPTIONS   judgment, changeable, argument

3. The root word doesn't change if it is preceded by a prefix.

   ▶ misshapen, disbelief, excommunicate

4. British and American spellings differ for some words.

   ▶ theater (American), theatre (British)

   ▶ honor (American), honour (British)

   ▶ realize (American), realise (British)

   ▶ canceled (American), cancelled (British)

   In your paper, use American spelling throughout, except when you are quoting from British sources, in which case you must retain the spellings of the original source.

Refer to the rules below when forming plurals:

1. Form the plural of most nouns by adding *-s* to the noun. Add an *-es* to nouns that end in *-ch*, *-s*, *-sh*, and *-x*.

   ▶ sailboat, sailboats; church, churches

2. Form the plural of most words that end in *-y* by changing the *-y* to *i* and adding *-es*, except when the *-y* is preceded by a vowel. Just add *-s* to proper names ending in *-y*.

   ▶ variety, varieties; donkey, donkeys; Mary, Marys

3. Form the plural of most words ending in *-o* by adding *-s*. However, if the *-o* is preceded by a consonant, add *-es*.

   ▶ radio, radios; potato, potatoes

4. Add an *-s* to the main word of a hyphenated compound word to form its plural.

   ▶ mothers-in-law, jacks-of-all-trade

5. Words that are derived from other languages sometimes retain the plural of the original language.

   ▶ chateau, chateaux; lied, lieder

34c Improving Your Spelling

Determine how you can best improve your spelling. Different people learn spelling in different ways. Some find that saying a word out loud and then writing it down helps. Others find that doing a spell check and then mentally sounding out the correct word before directing the computer to insert the word can help. Still other people like to develop mnemonic devices, or memory aids, such as these: *principal* ends in *-pal* because the principal is your *pal*; *independent* has *depend* in it.

One suggestion is to keep a log of your frequently misspelled words. Do not include difficult words with which everyone has trouble. Rather, start with basic words that you have trouble spelling. Note any patterns in the errors you make.

Note: Many word-processing programs, including Microsoft® Word 6.0, allow you to add words to a customized dictionary as you run the spell checker.

Tracking Your Spelling Demons   ONLINE TIP

All word processors have sophisticated, helpful, but imperfect spell checkers. Such programs will catch many misspellings and typos but will not detect those instances in which you have used the wrong word—for example, *there* instead of *their*. Keep a file of your spelling demons. As the final step for any writing project, use the Search function in your word processor to find these troublesome words in the context of your work.

34d Frequently Misspelled Words

You may find it helpful to memorize a list of frequently misspelled words, such as the following:

absence	achievement	aggravate	analyze
academic	acknowledge	all right	answer
accidentally	acquaintance	a lot	apparently
accommodate	acquire	altogether	appearance
accomplish	across	amateur	appropriate
accumulate	address	among	argument

arithmetic
arrangement
ascend
athlete
athletics
attendance
audience
basically
beginning
believe
benefited
Britain
bureau
business
cafeteria
calendar
candidate
cemetery
changeable
characteristic
chosen
column
commitment
committed
committee
comparative
competitive
conceivable
conference
conferred
conqueror
conscience
conscientious
conscious
courteous
criticism
criticize
curiosity
dealt
decision
definitely
descendant
describe
description
despair

desperate
develop
dictionary
disappear
disappoint
disastrous
dissatisfied
eighth
eligible
embarrass
eminent
emphasize
entirely
environment
equivalent
especially
exaggerated
exhaust
existence
experience
extraordinary
extremely
familiar
fascinate
February
foreign
forty
fourth
friend
government
grammar
guard
guidance
harass
height
humorous
illiterate
immediately
incredible
indefinitely
indispensable
inevitable
infinite
intelligence
interesting

irrelevant
irresistible
knowledge
laboratory
legitimate
license
lightning
loneliness
maintenance
maneuver
mathematics
mischievous
necessary
noticeable
occasion
occasionally
occur
occurred
occurrence
optimistic
original
outrageous
pamphlet
parallel
particularly
pastime
performance
permissible
perseverance
perspiration
phenomenon
physically
picnicking
playwright
politics
practically
precede
precedence
preference
preferred
prejudice
primitive
privilege
probably
proceed

professor
prominent
pronunciation
quiet
quite
receive
recommend
reference
referred
religion
repetition
restaurant
rhythmical
rhythm
roommate
schedule
secretary
seize
separate
sergeant
several
siege
similar
sincerely
sophomore
subtly
succeed
surprise
temperature
thorough
tragedy
transferred
truly
unnecessarily
until
usually
vacuum
vengeance
villain
weird
whether
writing

GRAMMAR INDEX

INDEX

Entries in *italics* appear in the Usage Glossary (pages 121–30).
Entries in **boldface** appear in the Glossary of Computer-Based Writing Terms (pages 201–4).

GLOSSARY OF COMPUTER-BASED WRITING TERMS

ASCII (pronounced "ASS-key"; originally an acronym for the American Standard Code for Information Interchange). A widely accepted code for assigning numbers to the letters of the alphabet. ASCII files contain only text, with no formatting information, and thus can be easily moved between different programs.

Bandwidth. The speed at which digital material can be sent to a computer connection, at home usually through a modem and telephone line. In 1997, the fastest connection available to most home computers was 56,000 bits per second (shortened to 56 bps), fast enough to download a 10-page paper in a couple of seconds, but some 150 times too slow for full-screen, full-motion video.

Boolean. A strategy for searching the Web or electronic databases generally using terms such as *and* or *or* to expand or narrow a search.

Browser. Software such as Navigator from Netscape or Internet Explorer from Microsoft for reading through vast amounts of material available on the World Wide Web.

Bullet. A graphical character (typically, ●) usually placed before each item in an unnumbered list.

Client. A software program that runs on a personal computer and that is designed to share information on a regular basis (via the Internet or another network connection) with a central computer (or server).

Cyberspace. A term, coined by author William Gibson in his novel *Neuromancer*, that refers to the entire range of resources available through computer networks.

Default. The predefined settings that a program assumes unless instructed otherwise.

Directory. A listing of the files on a disk collected in one specific area. Subdirectories are collections of files organized under other directories or subdirectories.

Em dash. A solid dash the equivalent of the width of the letter *M*. (On a typewriter, two hyphens would be used instead.)

FAQ (Frequently Asked Questions). Documents widely distrib-

uted on the Internet that list and answer common questions
on particular subjects.

Fixed fonts. Character sets like those found on typewriters
where each letter, number, punctuation mark, symbol, and
space occupies the same width as every other character.

Flush left and flush right. A command that aligns text on
the left or right margin, respectively.

Font. All the characters of a given size and design of type.

Footer. Text, with or without a page number, that appears below the bottom margin of all pages or of every other page.

Format. (1) To prepare a blank disk for receiving information;
(2) to organize the layout of a printed page, especially regarding size, style, type, margins, and so forth.

Hanging margin (also called **hanging indent**). A paragraph style in which the first line begins flush left and all
subsequent lines are indented (as in this glossary and in a
standard Works Cited section).

Hard (nonbreaking) space. A space that, for the purpose of
line breaks, attaches itself to the following character.

Header. Text, with or without a page number, that appears
above the top margin of all pages or of every other page.

Home page. Generally refers to the opening page for a business, organization, or person on the World Wide Web. Home
pages introduce their subjects and normally contain links to
other pages at the same site and across the Web.

HTML (Hypertext Markup Language). The coding language
used to create hypertext documents for use on the World
Wide Web. HTML works by placing formatting and linking
instructions for browsers within angled brackets, all inside
plain text (ASCII) files.

Hypertext documents. Screens of online textual and graphical information connected by multiple links. The hypertext
version of a standard literary work would have a wealth of
secondary information about the work and the author all
linked to the primary text; hypertext fiction would have multiple narrative paths much like an interactive adventure
game.

Internet (the Net). The vast collection of computers throughout the world, connected to each other mostly over leased
telephone lines and all using the same set of standards (called
protocols) for sharing information. Increasingly, the term is
not being capitalized.

ISP (Internet Service Provider). A business or service offered by
a school that provides dial-up access to the Internet. ISPs have

to provide a telephone line and modem at their end for each of their customers who is attached to the Internet at the same time.

ustified. A margin where each line is flush with the line above it; it is created by adjusting the space between words.

andscape. A rectangular page that is wider than it is tall, as in a typical landscape painting. See *portrait*.

ocal area network (**LAN**; also called **ethernet network**). A system in which computers are directly linked together in a single room, office, or building so that they can share files, hard-disk space, and printers.

og in. To inform a network program that you are online and ready to send and receive information.

ewsgroups. A formal collection of groups organized via Listserv programs; a colorful, informal part of the Internet that permits users with special interests (on almost anything) to communicate with each other by posting personal messages to a common electronic bulletin board. Various software programs allow individuals to subscribe to individual newsgroups from around the world.

aragraph margin. The left margin for the first line of a paragraph.

oint. The size of individual characters in a font, with 72 points per inch. The standard typing font is 12 points.

ortrait. A rectangular page that is taller than it is wide, as in a typical portrait painting. See *landscape*.

roportional spacing. A feature that assigns differing amounts of space to different characters—for example, *i* takes up less space than *w*.

agged margin. An uneven right-hand or left-hand margin, the result of a word processing program's use of a set space between all words.

ans serif. A typeface without cross strokes at the end of characters (this is sans serif type).

earch engine. A Website or service such as Alta Vista that attempts to index everything on the Web; users search the service's index and are then given direct links to Websites.

erif. A typeface with cross strokes at the end of characters (this is serif type).

oft hyphen. A temporary hyphen used to split a word between lines.

emplate file. A "master file," analogous to a printed form, with preset information and questions designed to be completed on many different occasions. As with a printed form,

one normally works with a copy of a template file, not th
original.

Typeface. The design features common to a complete famil
of fonts.

URL (an acronym for Uniform Resource Locator). The offici
description and address of a resource on the Internet.

Usenet. A largely informal arrangement for the sharing (
"news" on thousands of different topics among discussio
groups set up all over the world. Usenet makes all these di
cussions available in a single site.

Wide area network (WAN). The linking of LANs over larg
distances.

World Wide Web. A system by which much of the info
mation on the Internet is linked together, enabling users t
jump transparently from one item and physical location t
another.

WYSIWYG (pronounced "wizzywig"; an acronym for Wha
You See Is What You Get). A feature of a word processir
program that displays on screen essentially what a documer
will look like when printed.

Switchboard http://www.switchboard.com
*Allows Web browsers to look up the names, phone numbers, and street addresses of pe[...]
and businesses.*

Four 11 http://www.four11.com
Yahoo!'s white-pages directory.

INFOMINE http://lib-www.ucr.edu
*The University of California offers this comprehensive Internet resource containing da[...]
electronic journals, electronic books, online library catalogs, articles, and directories
pertaining to a variety of scholarly topics.*

BUBL LINK http://bubl.ac.uk/link
Offers a catalog of selected Internet resources.

Tile.net http://tile.net/lists
A reference to all the Listserv discussion groups on the Internet.

Deja News http://www.dejanews.com
Provides links to more than 50,000 Internet discussion forums.

WebCrawler http://www.webcrawler.com

Yahoo! http://www.yahoo.com

HotBot http://www.hotbot.com

InfoSeek http://www.infoseek.com

Alta Vista http://www.altavista.digital.com

Humanities http://humanitas.ucsb.edu
Offers academic and professional resources for humanities research.

Virtual Libraries Museums Page
http://www.comlab.ox.ac.uk/archive/other/museums.html
A comprehensive directory of online museums and museum-related resources.

History Sites by Time Period http://www.tntech.edu/www/acad/hist/period.ht[...]
Provides resources in history and is maintained by the Tennessee Technological Unive[...]

H-Net: Humanities and Social Sciences http://www.h-net.msu.edu
Provides information and resources for research in the humanities and social sciences.

World Wide Arts Resources http://wwar.com
A comprehensive gateway to the arts on the Internet for arts enthusiasts and professio[...]

Guide to Philosophy on the Internet http://www.earlham.edu/~peters/philink[...]
*Provides access to the Hippias search engine, which offers comprehensive coverage of
philosophy sites.*

American Studies Web http://www.georgetown.edu/crossroads/index.html
*The American Studies crossroads project contains pedagogical, scholarly, and instituti[...]
information for the American studies community.*

American Studies at the University of Virginia http://xroads.virginia.edu
*A gathering of American studies resources, including an annotated directory, hypertex[...]
projects, and cultural maps.*

Literature and Writing http://www.stlawu.edu/library.http/sp-eng.eng.html#1w[...]
St. Lawrence University Libraries offer this catalog of resources in literature and writin[...]

Literary Resources on the Net http://www.english.upenn.edu/~jlynch/Lit
*Maintained by the University of Pennsylvania, the site offers a catalog of literary reso[...]
the Web.*